Er

"*Let It Shine!* by Martha and Greg Singleton will inspire parents to see their children as the world changers God created them to be and to equip them to live the greatest adventure on earth— following Christ and His purpose for their lives. Love this book —it's a must-read for moms, dads, and those who work with today's children."—**Cheri Fuller**, speaker and author of *Mother-Daughter Duet, Raising Motivated Kids, The One Year Book of Praying Through the Bible,* and other books

"I've always thought that children come with a built-in mission. I call it a 'personalized, God-sized adventure.' Greg and Martha had that same thought and turned it into a book that's as unique, delight-ful, practical, and spiritually powerful as they are. With the decline of social values and the deterioration of the media, the darkness seems to get deeper and darker. *Let It Shine!* is a book for such a time as this, not just equipping parents but inspiring and enabling them to raise children that are deeply missional, yet full of life, laughter, and love."—**"Bongo Rod" Butler**, *The Coconut Hut Radio Show* and *The Brilliant Adventures of Captain FlashLight*

Other books in this series:

Setting Up Stones:
A Parent's Guide to Making Your Home a Place of Worship

Let It Shine!

Partnering with God to Raise World Changers

Martha and Greg Singleton

NEW HOPE
PUBLISHERS
Birmingham, Alabama

New Hope® Publishers
P. O. Box 12065
Birmingham, AL 35202-2065
www.newhopepublishers.com
New Hope Publishers is a division of WMU®.

Library of Congress Cataloging-in-Publication Data

Singleton, Martha, 1949-
  Let it shine! : partnering with God to raise world changers / Martha and Greg Singleton.
    p. cm.
  Includes bibliographical references (p.   ) and index.
  ISBN 978-1-59669-275-6 (sc : alk. paper) 1. Child rearing--Religious aspects--Christianity. 2. Christian children--Religious life. 3. Discipling (Christianity) I. Singleton, Greg, 1952- II. Title.
  BV4529.S453 2011
  248.8'45--dc23
                              2011018069

ISBN-10: 1-59669-275-8
ISBN-13: 978-1-59669-275-6
N104138 • 0811 • 3M1

Dedication

To our parents,
Norma and Barney McMullan,
and Joanne and C. B. Singleton,
who made sure that we had music lessons
and library cards and tickets to sporting events and concerts,
who told us over and over that we were capable
of achieving any dream and, most important of all,
who introduced us to the One who created us
and gave His Son to die for us.
Your legacy is a blessing!

Table of Contents

Charlie Duke compares his mission to the moon to the adventure of following Christ. The story of his passion and courage sets the stage for parents to discover ways to direct children toward finding and following the Father's unique plan for each of their lives.

We all dream about what our children will be. The details for each child's calling are actually God's responsibility. A new look at the staple Scripture "train up a child" reveals that our foremost task is to create an appetite for following Jesus.

Missional—it's a concept that was born when Jesus issued to His followers the Great Commission. A look at that passage as it relates to children in general, and yours in particular, reveals the insight that, more than just ensuring their place in heaven, we are to nurture children to affect their world for God.

John 3:16 tells us that it was God's love that motivated Him to send His Son, Jesus. That love for people still motivates us to reach out today. A sincere love for people can't be taught. It's caught from parents who act it out in ways that are genuine, practical, and intentional.

Each person's attitudes or actions are a reflection of their need for God. While our young children might not be ready for the front lines, we must give attention to cultivating their hearts for God's lost ones.

Jesus taught us by example that prayer is essential to any mission. When parents pray, children learn its value. When parents pray intelligently, children learn its practicality. When parents pray intelligently and passionately, children learn its power.

The adage "Actions speak louder than words" is an important scriptural principle. Knowing that the ultimate example is Jesus' death on the Cross, we need to help our children learn that the world often won't give us the privilege of sharing the Word until we've won that right with our service.

THANK YOU ...

Blake Mycoskie, Samkon Gado, Sheryl Russell, Lindsay Reyes, Dr. Tony Campolo, Gen. Charlie Duke, McNair Wilson, Dr. Henry Blackaby, Dr. Lloyd Ogilvie, Pastor Andrae Crouch, and Bobby Jaklich, for trusting us with your stories.

Pete, Lydia and all the kids, Scott and Lori, Jeff, Ruth, Peter, Monica and Jazz, Peter, Kay and Maren, the Rogers family, Allen, Wanda, Jill, Kenn, Pat, Dede, Deborah, and Ted, our precious friends in faith, for sharing your lives, your ideas, and your stories with us.

New Hope Publishers, for a shared vision for our world and for doing all things with excellence.

Les Stobbe, for steering us through all the details prayerfully and with integrity.

Matt, Annie, Robbie, and Josiah for letting your lights shine in our family and in your worlds.

Introduction

Hide it under a bushel? No!
I'm gonna let it shine
Hide it under a bushel? No!
I'm gonna let it shine
Hide it under a bushel? No!
I'm gonna let it shine
Let it shine,
Let it shine,
Let it shine.

"This Little Light of Mine"
Public Domain/Traditional American Song

The voices of children singing this familiar song at the top of their lungs have echoed through Sunday School rooms for generations. Even though it's a kids' song, the message is vibrant and alive, validated by Jesus' declaration that children were the very essence of the kingdom of God. It purposefully challenges them to live a life that makes an impact on those around them. But the reality of today's culture tempers that challenge a bit. The world into which our children are called to bring a lifetime of light is inundated with darkness. Often our parental focus becomes simply to protect them, to make life easier and better for them, or just to make them happy. And though our intentions might be positive, sometimes our instructions and boundaries are motivated by fear and can actually hinder our children from maturing in their own exciting spiritual adventures.

In answering the high calling of parenting, we may find that God's goals for our children are directed in a surprisingly different direction from what we have assumed. So what does God actually expect from us when He blesses our home with a little one? This book is a Scripture-based study exploring specific attitudes and practices that will enable parents to encourage each child to discover and develop their personal, God-given purpose and become adept at using their individual gifts and abilities as God intends.

Between the book's chapters are sections entitled "Live It!," a collection of true stories in narrative format from various missional families and individuals. These stories are intended to inspire you to lead your family into bold new adventures of faith. Some of the stories will feature young men and women you know from the Bible. Some you might have heard of because they have recently made a mark on this world that has brought them special attention. And some of them are just people you might pass on the street, never knowing that they have embraced a lifestyle that, above all else, is focused on intensely following God and His mission for their lives.

Each chapter also includes guided self-examination and a section entitled "*Do* Try This at Home." Here you'll find ideas and prompts that will encourage your family's hands-on participation in walking with Christ in an adventure of faith.

We pray that the Holy Spirit will enlighten you and your family through the words we wrote here and that the Jesus light will shine through you and your children, impacting the world around you.

Not Another Book About Parenting

No one lights a lamp and hides it in a jar or puts it under a bed. Instead, he puts it on a stand, so that those who come in can see the light.
—Luke 8:16 (NIV)

Ten...nine...eight..."

"All I could think of was, How did I get here?" Charlie Duke said. On that morning of April 16, 1972, Charlie was strapped into *Apollo 16's* command module, atop the Saturn rocket on the launching pad at Cape Canaveral. This was his first flight as an astronaut. He had never even been propelled through earth's atmosphere into outer space before, but now he was on his way to the moon, over 500,000 miles away.

"Seven... six..."

While he was growing up, Charlie didn't dream about going to the moon. There was no NASA then and no astronaut program that a young person could dream about participating in. Charlie's heroes were men like his dad, the soldiers, and sailors who were fighting on World War II battlegrounds in Europe and the Pacific. He admired their character and their bravery, and he wanted to be one of them and serve his country. So he determined that he would go to the United States Naval Academy and prepare for a career as a military officer. While he was there, he discovered flying and knew he was meant to be a pilot. He quickly became one of the military's shining stars. In 1966 when the opportunity arose for Charlie to move into the space program, he was eager to become an astronaut. Six years later, he was on his way to the moon.

"Five...four..."

As Charlie listened to the countdown in his headphones, the adrenaline began to flow. This was the culmination of years of training. But this time it was not a simulation. It was the real thing. He wanted them to hurry, so there would be no chance to abort the mission before it could get off the ground.

"Three...two...one...we have liftoff."

Fantastic, thought Charlie. We're on our way. No turning back now. At ignition, he felt the spaceship shaking violently, the thrust required to get the rocket into orbit overwhelming the small capsule. What do astronauts do at liftoff? "This one," said Charlie, "was holding on for dear life! Had I not heard Mission Control, saying 'You're go, you're go,' I would have thought we were shaking to pieces, coming apart at the seams. It was like riding on a runaway freight train."

Despite what it felt like to Charlie, *Apollo 16* was performing flawlessly. It accelerated to 26,000 miles per hour, and it seemed to him that his heart was racing just as fast.

The moon was eight hours away, and it was getting larger and larger in the windows of the command module. Charlie could begin to see distinct craters and terrain. Soon, the ship settled into lunar orbit. Charlie and fellow astronauts John Young and Ken Mattingly were experiencing something that few in history ever had. "We were no longer serious," Charlie recalled. "We were just like exuberant little kids."

Charlie and John Young left the command module and fitted themselves into the even smaller lunar module, the spacecraft that would take them to the surface of the moon. The lunar module separated from the command module. Charlie would soon be on the moon.

The module drew closer and closer to the lunar surface. "I began to call out the landing point designation," said Charlie, "and John began to maneuver us to the south, our landing site, the Descartes Plains." They moved nearer and nearer to the moon. Lunar dust began to kick up around the spaceship.

Then, they made contact with the moon's surface. Charlie's first word from the moon was simple, but said volumes. "Wow!" Despite the challenges, the difficulties, and the fears, Charlie Duke had completed his mission.

In 1979 author Tom Wolfe wrote about the indefinable characteristics that made American astronauts willingly put their lives on the line for their mission. He called it the "right stuff." What was it that motivated these people to take huge risks in order to accomplish great things? What was it like for them growing up? What values did their parents instill in them that made them who they were?

There have been only 12 people in the history of mankind who took on the challenges of a lunar spaceflight and stepped onto the surface of the moon, and Charlie Duke is one of them. Charlie, like the other astronauts, knew the possibilities of failure involved in his mission. He accepted the idea that interplanetary exploration was a life-threatening adventure, but he was willing to take on the dangers. To him, the long-term results far outweighed the potential catastrophes.

> Charlie's first word from the moon was simple, but said volumes. "Wow!"

After the adventure of space exploration, Charlie Duke began to seek the next challenge. He found it in the mission that God had for him, living a life that made an eternal difference in others. For Charlie, the thrill of the journey to the moon was temporary. But he discovered that God's mission was a true adventure that had no comparison. "I used to say that I could live for ten thousand years and never have an experience as thrilling as walking on the moon," Charlie said. "But the excitement and the satisfaction of that walk doesn't begin to compare with my walk with Jesus, a walk that lasts forever!"

This is not just another book about parenting. But, before you get the idea that we're implying something derisive about that genre, you need to know how we really feel about it. Thank God for those Christian writers and teachers who have faithfully instructed and challenged parents in methods and principles. Those people helped us formulate how we would raise our children, and we believe wholeheartedly in the validity and effectiveness of their ministries. In fact, we've taught and written concerning parenting for the extent of our ministry. However, despite the section of the bookstore you found this book in, it's just not another book about parenting.

Parenting books focus on how you do what you do. They analyze the cause and effect of your parenting style, and how you should employ it to mold and shape your child's life. They teach you how to ensure your child will be successful and what you should do to maximize their accomplishments. They offer methodology about reining in your child's behavior, guiding their decisions, and providing protection from bad influences. Parenting books have been written about your child and church, your child and school, your child and sports, your child and music, your child and vacations and a myriad of other topics. All these subjects are necessary to discuss, important to implement and certainly worthy to be written about. But this book just doesn't fall into the same category.

This book is not about your perspective or even your child's point of view. This book is about God. It's all about what's in His heart and what's on His mind. This is about our participation in His unique, personal mission for us, and how we can make the mission attractive to each member of our family. It's about preparing the way for our child to change their world.

Occasionally, our very best efforts in parenting, as sincere as they may be, might actually hinder what God has in mind, even being counterproductive to His plans for the life of the child that He has entrusted to us. As engaged as we become in how we raise our children, and as sincerely as we desire to do all the right things, sometimes we still miss the mark. Our focus on what being a parent really is about can actually become clouded by our own enthusiasm for the task to be accomplished. Sometimes our expectations for our kids are colored by our own missed opportunities. And perhaps even our fears become the motivation that directs our parental decisions.

At times, we may have overstepped our responsibilities and taken upon ourselves the task of programming data into our child's life that might even clash with God's purposes. Our view is often clouded by the culture and our own experience. Our desire is that we don't want our kids to make the same mistakes we made. Or, perhaps we want them to reach higher and work harder to accomplish something that we ourselves may have failed to achieve. Although that might be an admirable focus, it's probably not the goal that God has in mind. We shake our heads at the tales of cheerleader moms or overbearing Little League dads, but it's all too easy to fall into the same traps as we lead our children spiritually.

We want that baby to be successful when she grows up, so we input all the "successful" attributes that we can think of. We want him to want for nothing, and we strive to protect him from having to go through difficult situations. Of course, she should have the very best educational opportunities, make all the contacts that will move her along in her career and, if we arrange things just right, she'll marry someone who's worthy of her, and they'll live happily ever after. That's a very pretty story. But the gifts that God placed within His creation of life and the plan that He has for that child might require a different pathway.

Often our fears become the motivation that directs our parental decisions. The world we live in today is frightening and dangerous. But, in our desire to protect the precious gift that God has given to us, we might find that we're actually sheltering our kids from the very challenges that make them strong and give them courage.

As the old saying goes, if you want to hear God laugh, tell Him your plans. Our view of ourselves, and our lives, and of our children and their futures, is shaded by our ability to see only the limited background that we have along with the moment where we now find ourselves. God sees eternity. As personal as He is with every human being that He has created, He views each of us within the context of time: past, present, future and forever. From His vantage point, He is not only able to see every detail of that individual child's journey, but also his relationship to the rest of the universe and all of time. It's mind blowing to think about but, after all, He is God and His methods and abilities are far beyond ours.

Consistent with the adventure of faith He has for all of us, God's ideas about parenting are a lot like walking a tightrope. He expects us to balance the careful sheltering and direction we provide with the open-handed understanding that this child's life is His project. So we seek information and education that will ensure that we will make all the right parenting decisions. We read books, listen to DVDs, attend workshops, and do all the admirable tasks to enlighten us about our responsibility. We reason that if we can accumulate enough parental schematics then we might be able to figure this whole thing out. That's exactly how focused and intense our approach to parenting should be.

But all the solutions won't automatically be found in volume after volume of complicated and detailed philosophies. As dedicated as we are to the task of collecting all the information that we can accumulate about "how to," it just won't give us a clear understanding of what each individual child's life should look like. God wants our kids to have the "right stuff" for His mission. A series of formulas and outlines may not bring the results He desires. His guidelines for being a parent are probably much more concise than we would expect. In every "kid package" God has included a small instruction sheet that contains only one simple sentence: "Prepare this child for his mission!"

THINK

▲ How would I describe my parenting style?

▲ How do I view my responsibilities as a parent?

▲ What are my priorities for my child and how did I arrive at them?

DO TRY THIS AT HOME!

❏ Movie night! Schedule a family movie night, complete with popcorn, and watch one of the many great movies that have themes of adventure and mission. Be sure to find one that is age-appropriate for your kids. At www.pluggedinonline.com, www.dove.org, and preview.gospelcom.net, you can find reviews to assist you with your search for movies with family-friendly content. Following the movie, be sure your family discusses any pertinent themes. This is primarily a time to let the kids talk, rather than a time for parents to teach a lesson.

❏ Reading out loud to your kids provides not only a great way to connect with them, but it has been proven to provide an educational edge. Be sure to talk about what you read, too, making application of life lessons into your children's lives. With books like C. S. Lewis's *The Chronicles of Narnia*, you can create many evenings of excitement and enlightenment in your home.

✎ There's a new term that describes overly possessive, overly protective parents: *helicopter parents*. Use Google or another search engine to find this term. Take a personal inventory, to see if there might be ways that you are, either spiritually or emotionally, overly protective of your child.

■ ■ ■ LIVE IT! ■ ■ ■

Daniel, Hananiah, Mishael, and Azariah had met like this many times before. Their friendship had been the source of many good times during their lives but, almost as often, they provided support and accountability for each other.

Now they were facing, together, one of those difficult times. It was one of those situations that had forced them to grow up quickly, calling for some mature decisions that most people their age were never required to make.

"We have to draw a line somewhere," Daniel exclaimed. "There's a point where we will be compromising everything that we've been taught to believe in."

Azariah agreed. "That's right. To think it all started with changing our Hebrew names. Shadrach, Meshach, Abednego, and Belteshazzar—I still can't get used to that."

"Yeah, but we agreed we could live with that," said Hananiah. "This is not acceptable at all, though. We have to take a stand here."

The room was now quiet as the young men considered the cost of taking such a stance against Nebuchadnezzar. The Babylonian king had commanded everyone, including the captive Hebrews, to bow down before a huge golden image. If anyone failed to worship the idol, the sentence was death. The commandments that Moses had brought to the Hebrews generations before were completely clear, especially: "You shall not make for yourself an idol." The king's order would require that these young men break that commandment. And, that was something that they would not do.

After Babylon had conquered Israel, Nebuchadnezzar knew that the best way to maintain order would be to assimilate the Hebrews into his culture. So he gathered the brightest and strongest young

Hebrews and began to indoctrinate them. Daniel, Hananiah, Mishael, and Azariah were the cream of the crop.

Because these young men were so talented and so diligent in taking on the tasks they had been assigned, people took notice. Most of the Babylonian authorities were willing to turn their heads to some of the quirky elements of their Hebrew culture. These boys had the potential to be an example to all the other Israelites.

Daniel, Hananiah, Mishael, and Azariah knew that once they refused to bow down before the idol, all the favor that had been lavished upon them would be gone. They understood that when their faith in Jehovah God was exposed in such a public manner, others of their kinsmen would be encouraged to steel themselves against Nebuchadnezzar's heavy hand.

The young men went on their way, attending to the responsibilities of their positions, but determined that they would never compromise their faith. On the first day that the decree went into effect, the music blared out across the city, signaling the call to worship the golden idol. Every citizen within earshot fell to the ground, worshipping Nebuchadnezzar and his statue. The young men were conspicuous in their refusal to bow down. And some of the Babylonian officials, who were jealous of the privileges that had been granted the boys, spotted three of them, Hananiah, Mishael and Azariah, standing tall. They couldn't wait to blow the whistle on them.

King Nebuchadnezzar was livid. How dare they show him up like this after all he had done for them! "Fire up the furnace as hot as you can get it," Nebuchadnezzar yelled through clenched teeth. "I won't tolerate this."

Soldiers seized Hananiah, Mishael, and Azariah and brought them before the king. "Are you serious? You actually refused to bow down?" he asked them. "You know what that means, don't you? What do you have to say for yourselves?" Nebuchadnezzar liked these boys. He secretly hoped that he could generate enough fear from his bluster that they would acquiesce to his wishes.

Mishael looked right into Nebuchadnezzar's eyes and said, "King, we don't have to defend ourselves. Our God is our defense. He will protect us from the fire."

The young men were tied up and thrown into the furnace. It was so hot that the soldiers who got close to the fire died on the spot when they threw the prisoners in.

Nebuchadnezzar dared to come closer and look into the fire. He was astonished by what he saw. "Didn't we only throw those three in there?" he asked those around him. "I see four people in there! They're all alive and walking around! And the fourth one looks like he could be the Son of God!"

What the Babylonians saw there frightened and amazed them. When Hananiah, Mishael, and Azariah were retrieved from the furnace, they were completely unharmed. They didn't even smell like smoke.

Though Nebuchadnezzar was shaken, he knew beyond any doubt that he had witnessed a miracle. "The God of those Hebrew boys is real!" he proclaimed. "He is so real that they were willing to give up their lives, and He protected them. Let everyone acknowledge and worship their God, the one true God!"

(Based on Daniel 3)

CHAPTER 2

Cookies
and
Olive Juice

But Jesus said, "Let the children come to me. Don't stop them! For the Kingdom of Heaven belongs to those who are like these children." And he placed his hands on their heads and blessed them before he left.
—Matthew 19:14–15 (NLT)

"Throughout the Scriptures, whenever God is ready to do something new, a baby is born."
—Dr. Henry Blackaby

Do you remember when you first held that baby in your arms? The rush of emotion at seeing that little bundle was equaled only by your thoughts of the future and that child's potential. Before you could even get the baby home from the hospital, all the dreams about tomorrow had already begun. You couldn't wait to see those first steps across the room or to hear those first words. The first day of school will be great. And won't it be exciting to see him on the baseball field? Just imagine what it will be like at her first dance recital. We begin to project our hopes and expectations on that new little one. Beyond the mundane, we might even design plans for how this life will serve God, envisioning successful ministry in our child's future. In our excitement and anticipation, we reason, "How awesome! God has presented me with a fresh new canvas here, and I'm going to create a classic work of art!"

It really would be so exciting if it was simply our responsibility to select all the colors and designs for that child's life and fill that canvas with beauty, just the way we had it pictured in our mind. Then we could frame it, hang it in a gallery somewhere, and the whole world would pass by and tell us what a wonderful job of parenting we had done. And when the audience applauds our efforts, we feel great!

But, this is the point where we need to slow down a bit. This isn't our art project. Despite the biology involved, this gift from God has nothing to do with what *we* can create. That baby isn't the product of our ingenuity and dedication to the craft of being a parent. Parenting really has very little to do with our credentials and successes. In fact, God has already invested His work and creativity in that child's life, before she was even born. David acknowledged God's masterful work in Psalm 139.

> *Oh yes, you shaped me first inside, then out;*
> *you formed me in my mother's womb.*
> *I thank you, High God—you're breathtaking!*
> *Body and soul, I am marvelously made!*
> *I worship in adoration—what a creation!*
> *You know me inside and out,*
> *   you know every bone in my body;*
> *You know exactly how I was made, bit by bit,*
> *   how I was sculpted from nothing into something.*
> *Like an open book, you watched me grow from conception to birth;*
> *   all the stages of my life were spread out before you,*
> *The days of my life all prepared*
> *   before I'd even lived one day.*
> *—Psalm 139:13–16 (*The Message*)*

What a masterpiece that child is! The care and attention to detail that we can offer is nothing compared to what God has already done and what he plans to do throughout the future. His thoughts and designs for that life far surpass ours. The same Almighty God who created the indescribable beauty and vastness of the universe, focused the same power and wisdom on one being and made your child.

He has other ideas about what our role is supposed to be. When He graciously places a baby in our home, there is absolutely nothing lacking. What God asks of parents is that we discover all that He has invested in that child and direct those abilities and proclivities toward maturity. Our task is to discern the valuable gifts that God has placed there and enhance that beauty all for His glory. Then that person, our child, can realize the potential that God had intended from the very beginning of time.

Our natural tendency is to think of that baby as "ours." From the minute we peer through the nursery window and proudly point out which little bundle belongs to us, we are swept up in a sort of pride of ownership. Just look at how silly we act when "our" child is on the stage in a PTA program or when "my son" scores a basket.

Every coach and drama teacher has had to deal with parents who want to argue (or have the teacher's head on a platter) because their child did not get the starting position or the lead in the school play.

It is as if "our" kids are just detachable extensions of ourselves, and what they achieve is somehow our own. Perhaps that's why we never see bumper stickers that proclaim: "My child is inmate #FP6079850 at Simon Legree Federal Prison."

How startling it is to one day look into that youngster's eyes and realize that this child is a unique human being with hopes and dreams and thoughts that are totally separate from your own.

We never own our children. They are God's from the very beginning, entrusted to our care for the purpose of guiding each one to his or her own separate, personal relationship with Him.

So we should probably view our job more as that of a refiner rather than an artist. A refiner does sweaty work, and there's usually a lot of intense labor involved. Refineries follow a process that creates a valuable resource out of a raw material that already has an inherent worth. It doesn't happen quickly. It requires constant attention, and if any part of the process is overlooked or shortchanged, then the entire product could lose its usefulness and value. The process is extreme and the noise, the workspace, and the tasks involved are sometimes stressful and uncomfortable. Extreme pressure produces the value of diamonds. Intense heat creates efficient fuel. A refiner's work takes place in a setting that in no way resembles an artist's studio, but the refiner's job is necessary to bring out the beauty and the usefulness of the final products. Proverbs 22:6 is a familiar promise:

Train a child in the way he should go, and when he is old he will not turn from it.
— Proverbs 22:6 (NIV)

A significant amount of discussion has gone on about this simple verse. It has become the cornerstone of purposeful parental philosophies when a brand-new baby is born into a family. Their dreams for their child's well-being are contained in its truth. "If I can only do this right," they reason, "then this baby will most certainly grow up to love God and be a successful and productive member of society."

Many parents have clung to it as a glimmer of hope when an older child has turned their back on their faith. They recite its words almost like a mantra, and embrace its significance and truth, especially when things look dimmest. It comforts them and provides strength when there seems that there is absolutely nothing else available.

Unfortunately, some have even used this little verse to point an accusing finger at those same hurting parents, as if they had failed in pushing all the right child-rearing buttons. They wield it as if it were a weapon, beating down the wounded, and punishing them with an "I-told-you-so" attitude.

Some have proclaimed that this verse is foundational, the answer to everything. Others, though, have written it off as simply a nice idea or a pleasant thought that offers very little.

A person's first thought might be that this Scripture promises that good parenting will result in good behavior. Unfortunately, many parents, pastors and youth leaders in the last half century or so in America have focused so much time and energy on trying to ensure that their kids are "good" that they have lost sight of the fact that God did not create people simply to be good. He created them for a mission, to be used by Him to further His kingdom.

Proverbs 22:6 seems uncomplicated, yet it is often misquoted, misunderstood, misinterpreted, and misappropriated. So, what real significance can we uncover here? At the very least, the Truth revealed in this verse provides an uncluttered picture of God's ideas about what He wants from both you and your child. We just have to examine one pertinent phrase in order to take a close, honest look at what He's really telling us.

God's first instruction in the verse is, "Train up your child." Hebrew mothers practiced a method that taught their brand new babies the sucking action so that they could be well nourished. They dabbed olive juice or date juice on their finger and then rubbed it on the palate of the baby's mouth. The procedure would produce a sucking response and, soon, the baby would be trained to react with that response whenever it was time to be fed. It became a conditioned reflex, so natural to the baby that it became a part of who he was.

This training was probably what Proverbs 22:6 intends for us to notice. It involved a parent's dedication to the task at hand and an intentional and consistent process that would bring the baby to achieving the desired results.

Training a child is not only a discipline for the child. It's even more of a discipline for the parents. The ultimate goal is to develop an adult who is seeking and fulfilling God's personal purposes for his life. It's not our task to determine how that will look or what form we'd like it to take. Our task is to encourage a lifestyle that's ingrained from an almost habitual practice of following Him and knowing Him. That direction is a result of a parent's tireless effort to direct and redirect their child to God for wisdom, purpose, help, and inspiration.

This is not going to be accomplished, though, through mere instruction. And, while discipline and correction are necessary in your child's life, those are not the elements that will give her a heart that eagerly accepts her mission.

> Just like the Hebrew mother trained her child, parents need to create . . . that hunger

Just like the Hebrew mother trained her child, parents first need to create within their child that hunger for God. And that can't happen unless that child can taste it for himself.

Have you ever met a kid that didn't love chocolate chip cookies? Check that. Have you ever met *anybody* that didn't love chocolate chip cookies? Chocolate chip cookies aren't just the ultimate comfort food—they're an experience! And, that's how we all became chocolate chip cookie lovers. The bustle in the kitchen when Mom bakes the cookies draws attention to the fact that something is happening. The refrigerator and cabinet doors are opening and closing. There is the crash and clatter of pans and spoons. Then, it isn't long before that smell begins wafting through the house. There's nothing that compares to that delicious smell! By the time the cookies are done, there's such a hunger built up that nobody will be able to deny the cookie monster within us from at least a sample. And, when that first bite crosses our lips, it really might be the closest thing to heaven here on earth! The warm crunch, the sweet taste, keeps us coming back for them again and again. But as hard as we might try to describe the chocolate chip cookie experience to others, words mean nothing until they've actually had the opportunity to taste the cookies.

That's the way it is when we try to describe to our kids the joy that's found in following Christ and the fulfillment in taking on His mission. Words, rules, and platitudes can't make them want what God wants for them. So we have to create the experience for them and let them taste it for themselves.

The chapters that follow will examine what we need to do to generate an atmosphere in our homes that will produce that hunger in our kids. What they see flowing from the lives of their parents, how they respond to God's mission, and how they feel about other people is the result of that atmosphere. That's how they taste it. And if the flavor of what we offer is genuine and wholehearted, our children will want more. We will know that the training has been successful when their desire to follow God becomes almost a conditioned reflex. Then, their response to its taste will be like the psalmist David's.

> *I watch my step, avoiding the ditches and ruts of evil so I can spend all my time keeping your Word. I never make detours from the route you laid out; you gave me such good directions. Your words are so choice, so tasty; I prefer them to the best home cooking.*
> —Psalm 119:101–103 (*The Message*)

From teaching the infant to walk and talk to the place that, as an adult, she begins a family of her own and starts the cycle all over again, we are preparing her to hear God, follow His ways, and diligently obey His voice. Within that span of years, God reveals His plans within the heart and soul of the child that He created. As parents, our role is that of a conduit. We are there to provide the primary connection from the Creator to the heart and the mind of the one that He has called. We provide the environment where that can happen and then demonstrate the satisfaction found in its flavor.

Through the process of their growing up, it's often difficult to remember that the child is actually His chosen vessel, called for a unique purpose and mission in this world. Episodes of childish irresponsibility or moments of frailty and vulnerability tend to overshadow that big picture. So we get distracted. We get all wrapped up in what we have to do to make that child a productive member of society with the potential to be successful. As parents, we feel obligated to shield our children from difficult experiences at all costs. Yet, God is simply asking us to press through all the distractions of life and introduce them to Him.

<hr>

THINK

▲ What might I be taking for granted about my child's relationship with Christ?

▲ Am I taking on God's responsibilities in any areas of my child's relationship with Him?

▲ Do I ever view my parenting role as my project instead of God's work through me?

<hr>

DO TRY THIS AT HOME!

❏ This Is My Story
Set aside some time over a series of days or even weeks to gather your family, and let each parent tell the story of their own journey with God from childhood to the present. Invite each child to tell their story or ask questions of their parents, but don't pressure them. Make it a pleasant, easy and open discussion.

<hr>

LIVE IT!

"She's gorgeous!" Hegal exclaimed. "Her face, her hair, her figure, everything about her—she's absolutely breathtaking."

One of Hegal's assistants watched Esther walk across the courtyard. With his eyes glued on her, he wanted to know more about this beauty. "Who is she?" he asked his boss. "Do we know anything about her family or where she came from?"

"It doesn't matter, does it? She's just exactly King Xerxes' type."

"You're right about that. She's every bit as beautiful as Queen Vashti, but she's young and inexperienced. We can control her."

They underestimated Esther. Her intelligence, her courage, and her godly character were even more impressive than her beauty.

As a little girl, Esther didn't fantasize about becoming a princess or a queen. After she had been ordered to move into the palace, she was offered the very finest comforts and advantages in preparation for her marriage, but she refused them. Even after King Xerxes had selected her to be his wife, the Queen of Persia, Esther was apprehensive. She had a secret that nobody could know. Her name was really Hadassah, and she was a Jew.

She sought advice from the person she trusted most, the man who had raised her. Her uncle, Mordecai, was in hiding. He had angered Persian officials by refusing to bow down to them, and he now found himself targeted for hanging.

"Uncle Mordecai, isn't there some way that we can escape from this place and be free of all this?"

"Esther," answered Mordecai, "I believe that Jehovah has scripted this entire story and has chosen you to be the star! Our people are oppressed under the heavy hand of Persian rule. Haman, Xerxes' henchman, has even ordered the eradication of the Hebrew race. You are our only hope!"

"I long to worship God freely there in the palace, but I believe that may be impossible. Xerxes and his men watch every move I make."

Mordecai sighed, "My dear, innocent Esther. The attention you're receiving is not distrust. Xerxes and all the men around him are taken by your beauty."

"I just don't feel good about deceiving them about my identity. Most of all, though, I want to please Jehovah."

"You've found favor, Esther. Xerxes is pleased with you because you're everything Queen Vashti was not—respectful, honorable, and diligent. Just continue doing what you have been. God will use you there."

Weeks passed, and Haman was closing in on Mordecai. Haman was ambitious and would go to any extreme to exalt himself. His nefarious dealings and trifling deception were beginning to wear on everyone, even King Xerxes.

"Xerxes, I will give you ten thousand talents of silver if you'll allow me to get rid of the Hebrews," whined Haman. "We'll all be better off without them."

"I don't want your money; I just want peace! If I give you permission, will you let me rest?"

Haman shivered with excitement at this new bestowal of power. "Your majesty, I will leave your presence and fulfill your command."

When word of the planned genocide came to Esther, she knew the time had come for drastic action. Courageously, she decided to do the unimaginable. Without first asking permission, she would enter the king's chambers, reveal her true identity, and plead for the lives of her people.

"Xerxes, I must talk to you now."

"Of course, my queen. Come in! What's wrong?"

"I am not who you think I am," Esther said, her voice trembling. "My name is Hadassah, and I am Hebrew. You have given permission to Haman to destroy me, my family, and my entire race."

Immediately, Xerxes knew that Haman had deceived him. He loved Esther, and Haman's plot would not only rid Persia of the Hebrews, but also his beloved queen. The king was livid. "Hang Haman from the very gallows that he has prepared for Mordecai!"

Because of her wisdom and her courage, Xerxes granted Esther's request to save her people. He also gave Mordecai all the authority that had been held by Haman. "And, this day," the king proclaimed, "all the Jews are granted permission to worship their God and enjoy all the privileges granted all other citizens of Persia."

(Based on the Book of Esther)

CHAPTER 3

Please Pass The Salt

Let me tell you why you are here. You're here to be salt-seasoning that brings out the God-flavors of this earth. If you lose your saltiness, how will people taste godliness?
—Matthew 5:13 (*The Message*)

Missional. Your spell-check will probably call your hand on this word. *Missional* may be just now finding its way into the most current lexicon, but its definition was set into motion as Jesus gave His disciples their most important set of instructions.

Then the eleven disciples went to Galilee, to the mountain where Jesus had told them to go. When they saw him, they worshiped him; but some doubted. Then Jesus came to them and said, "All authority in heaven and on earth has been given to me. Therefore go and make disciples of all nations, baptizing them in the name of the Father and of the Son and of the Holy Spirit, and teaching them to obey everything I have commanded you. And surely I am with you always, to the very end of the age."
—Matthew 28:16–20 (NIV)

The unexpected usually is uncomfortable. That's how it was when Jesus gave His disciples the Great Commission, and that's how it is for us today. Whenever we're stretched or our sense of security is shaken, we tend to seek the path of least resistance. Jesus' challenge to His disciples and to us is not an easy task. He instructs us to change the world. That's an admirable goal, and hardly any of us would deny that it's something we would really want to do. But when that idea becomes reality, and when it calls for our active participation, we can pull up any number of reasons why it's inconvenient.

So is this a treatise on evangelism, "packing the pew," and the "Roman Road to Salvation"? Evangelism, the way we've known it, has had its time and served its purpose admirably, but the world we live in today has changed dramatically. Evangelism that's fueled by scorekeeping of how many we've witnessed to this week is met with skepticism in this culture. People wonder just what we're up to; they try to figure out what our real motivation might be. The perception that we're involved in a religious round-up is likely to make people suspicious rather than receptive.

Consider this true story about two people who both had a message they wanted people to hear. It took place at a Christian college, in a dormitory filled with freshman guys. The first messenger was a guy whose job was to drum up business for the pizza place just off campus. He would meet and greet people as they came into the lobby and present them with a big smile, a good word, and a coupon for $2 off a large pizza. He would proceed, every day, to make his way down the hallway, knock on doors, and introduce himself to the residents. He became a fixture in that freshman dorm. He called guys by name and got to know something about them, such as what they were majoring in or if they had a date lined up for Friday night. Everyone knew who he was, and he was someone they enjoyed seeing, especially after a rough day, because he always had a word of encouragement for them, along with that pizza coupon.

Messenger #2 understood his mission to be evangelizing anyone in that dorm who had not yet made a commitment to Christ. It was certainly a worthy calling, much more important than selling pizza, but his efforts were somewhat misguided. Nobody in the dorm knew who was responsible for it, but every day as they returned from classes they found a gospel tract shoved under each door in the dorm. Those stealth tactics continued for an entire semester. Who was more successful in getting their message across? Whose efforts were more to the point?

Being missional in the twenty-first century is not yesterday's evangelism, rehashed, reformed, and reworked. It has nothing to do with putting another notch in our gospel gun barrel. A missional message is relevant to where people of today's culture are living, in the midst of their struggles and their hopelessness. We are called not just to talk about our faith but to have a lifestyle that reflects Christlike attitudes and activities. The world wants to see authenticity from our lives. They are not impressed with how well we pretend we have it all together, but they want to know how Christ in us makes a difference when we're faced with adversity and difficulty.

> We should rethink some methods that may have once been good and right.

Too often, we have assumed that we have a right to demand attention, that our mission's portfolio included some kind of license to impose our thoughts and beliefs upon anyone we could corner. If we ever had that privilege, it's not available to us now. In our interactions in contemporary society, we must earn the opportunity to be heard.

So what does the Great Commission look like in this culture? Jesus' instructions to us are certainly as relevant today as they were on the mountain, but in order for the message to be compelling in today's world, we should rethink some methods that may have once been good and right, but are now simply our spiritual security blankets.

Our mission calls for action. From what Matthew 28 reveals about that day on the mountain, the disciples weren't really prepared for what Jesus was telling them. The enormity of the fact that He had overcome death and the grave was their focus. Was this really Jesus and was it really possible that He was alive again? Logic would follow that after such a victory as this, He would assuredly be setting up His kingdom now. And they knew when that happened they would be in line to reap the benefits that being part of the ruling inner circle would bring. But, rather than ease and privilege, Jesus was calling for action. Every verb in His commission called for intentional response and movement— "go," "make," "baptize," "teach." Had anyone there reasoned that this meeting was the climax of a beautiful story, his perception was erroneous. It was, instead, the start of what their walk with Christ would now look like, and what ours would look like today.

Jesus' focus has seldom been on the conclusion, more often it is on the starting point. The thing that makes our redemption story beautiful is how the beginning meshes with all that is to follow. Coming to Christ, our beginning, is a story of grace and mercy. He receives each of us with open arms, exactly the way we are. We can't do anything to earn His gift of salvation. We can't make ourselves righteous or clean enough. We come into the very presence of God with nothing to offer, with no task to complete other than coming to Him, seeking His salvation. And He restores us there, fills us with His Spirit, and begins the process of making us what He has created us to be.

But, that's only square one. It's true that, when we accept Him, someday we will live with Him forever in heaven, but that's not our focus now. We're not called to eternal rest and uninterrupted bliss until we breathe our last breath. It's at the starting point of our journey that Jesus lets us in on this family secret. Following Christ, day by day, is not safe or simple. Today, right now, He has called us to fulfill a mission—bringing light and life to every corner of the world where He's placed us. We can't do that merely by putting our heads together and tweaking our worship services or making our church facilities more comfortable. A missional lifestyle is active. It requires going and doing and being by everyone—man, woman, boy, and girl—who has decided to embark on the journey of walking with Christ. Who you are and where God has placed you is His calling on your life. Your home, your family, your work, your neighborhood and everywhere else that He leads you is your missions field.

Our mission requires relevance. Though there have been many doctrinal disagreements and denominational disputes throughout the centuries of church history, there is one area of agreement. The tried and true methodology of church tradition is that missionaries who minister in foreign lands must know the culture of the country where they will be living. It has always been understood that if a missionary's ignorance of the foreign culture caused them to offend someone, it would not only be counterproductive to ministry, it might even be dangerous! Paul addressed this issue in the church's earliest days.

If some unbeliever invites you to a meal and you want to go, eat whatever is put before you without raising questions of conscience.

But if anyone says to you, "This has been offered in sacrifice," then do not eat it, both for the sake of the man who told you and for conscience' sake—the other man's conscience, I mean, not yours. For why should my freedom be judged by another's conscience? If I take part in the meal with thankfulness, why am I denounced because of something I thank God for? So whether you eat or drink or whatever you do, do it all for the glory of God. Do not cause anyone to stumble, whether Jews, Greeks or the church of God— even as I try to please everybody in every way. For I am not seeking my own good but the good of many, so that they may be saved.
—1 Corinthians 10:27–33 (NIV)

It's necessary, if a missionary desires to be effective, that he be culturally relevant. He must understand the language and the customs of where he's living. He must be able to communicate truth that matters to the inhabitants of that particular missions field. In 1 Corinthians 9:22 Paul said, "I have become all things to all men, so that by all possible means I might save some." He was making the message relevant to the culture.

But suppose your missions field is not on some far away continent in an uncivilized village. A missional believer realizes that if God has called him to middle-class suburban America, the ability to understand the culture of those around him is just as necessary. Sometimes, what goes on in our own neighborhoods seems just as foreign to our Christian worldview as the pagan tribal rituals on the other side of the world might. And that can be frightening. So, we would be much more comfortable if we could just shut all that nonsense out.

But that is not Jesus' intention for us.

We are placed here for a purpose—to be salt and light, according to the Gospels. Fulfilling that purpose doesn't require that we blindly embrace baseless fads or willingly accept troublesome trends. But we need to know where to sprinkle the salt and where to shine the light. Pouring a box of salt into a culinary masterpiece ruins it, and blazing floodlights can be more irritating than helpful. Our mission is not to overwhelm everyone around us, nor does our task call for us to win an argument or force a response. Salt and light are enhancers, magnifying the inherent qualities of the place where they are used. As we engage our culture, we're not only called to reflect the grace and beauty of Jesus but, because He is constantly present, we are simply to reveal to those around us where He's already at work.

Our mission focuses on others. Though our mission calls for action, concentrating only on the tasks and the doing misses the point entirely. A missional lifestyle is not about us; it's all about others.

Jesus' disciples, James and John, came to Him with a request. They wanted to be the ones who sat on either side of Him, so that the attention that Jesus was receiving might spill over on them. Their perspective was so unlike Jesus', and so counterproductive to His message, that He had to call their hand on it.

> *Jesus called them together and said, "You know that those who are regarded as rulers of the Gentiles lord it over them, and their high officials exercise authority over them. Not so with you. Instead, whoever wants to become great among you must be your servant, and whoever wants to be first must be slave of all. For even the Son of Man did not come to be served, but to serve, and to give his life as a ransom for many."*
> —Mark 10:42–45 (NIV)

The most prominent aspect of Jesus' life was how He served others. His focus was on the meek, the sick, the poor, the hurting, and the lost. It was that very attitude that disturbed the religious leaders of His day. But He left no question about the emphasis of His ministry and the expectations that He had for those who chose to follow Him to have the same heart.

A missional heart has a passion for people. The great Protestant reformer, John Knox, prayed, "Lord, give me Scotland or I die!" That was real passion! The love that he had for the people of his country mirrored the mind of Christ. His calling was, above all else, to love and serve all people, from the beggars in the streets to the courts of the kings and queens. Ministry to our world can't be done without rubbing shoulders with people, seeing them face to face and accepting them, loving them just the way God loves them, and serving them right where they are as they are.

What does it look like to love and serve people in our missions field? Because every person's calling is different, exhausting every facet of that subject is impossible. How fortunate it is, then, that 1 Corinthians 13 offers us a beautiful pattern of what real love is. Possibly the last time you heard this chapter was in the context of a wedding ceremony. We often consider it when we're thinking about the love between a husband and a wife. Is it too far-fetched to think, though, that these verses should be the example that we look to when we want to know how Christ wants us to love everyone? A subtitle in *The Message* calls 1 Corinthians 13 "The Way of Love":

If I speak with human eloquence and angelic ecstasy but don't love, I'm nothing but the creaking of a rusty gate.

If I speak God's Word with power, revealing all his mysteries and making everything plain as day, and if I have faith that says to a mountain, "Jump," and it jumps, but I don't love, I'm nothing.

If I give everything I own to the poor and even go to the stake to be burned as a martyr, but I don't love, I've gotten nowhere. So, no matter what I say, what I believe, and what I do, I'm bankrupt without love.

Love never gives up.
Love cares more for others than for self.
Love doesn't want what it doesn't have.
Love doesn't strut,
Doesn't have a swelled head,
Doesn't force itself on others,
Isn't always "me first,"
Doesn't fly off the handle,
Doesn't keep score of the sins of others,
Doesn't revel when others grovel,
Takes pleasure in the flowering of truth,
Puts up with anything,
Trusts God always,
Always looks for the best,
Never looks back,
But keeps going to the end.

Love never dies. Inspired speech will be over some day; praying in tongues will end; understanding will reach its limit. We know only a portion of the truth, and what we say about God is always incomplete. But when the Complete arrives, our incompletes will be canceled.

When I was an infant at my mother's breast, I gurgled and cooed like any infant. When I grew up, I left those infant ways for good.

We don't yet see things clearly. We're squinting in a fog, peering through a mist. But it won't be long before the weather clears and the sun shines bright! We'll see it all then, see it all as clearly as God sees us, knowing him directly just as he knows us!

But for right now, until that completeness, we have three things to do to lead us toward that consummation: Trust steadily in God, hope unswervingly, love extravagantly. And the best of the three is love.
—1 Corinthians 13 (*The Message*)

How does this kind of love relate to your missions field? Can you love the people where you work with this kind of love? What about the people next door, or even that family in the next block that you don't particularly care for? The graceful, unselfish, giving kind of love that God is calling us to doesn't have an agenda. Even though our motivations might be good and our message might be true, love like this doesn't demand anything or expect to be heard. In fact, it listens much more than it talks. First Corinthians 13 love is cultivated through patience and growing relationships, rather than forcing the issues and trying to make things happen. It's nurtured when we serve others, when we reach out to the unlovable. It loves just like Jesus loves.

So how will our children learn about being missional? What can we do to teach them to desire that kind of lifestyle? We have to first understand that our primary missions field is within the walls of our home. Mom and Dad's calling is to live out the day-to-day practicalities of walking with Christ and demonstrate to their children what His love looks like. With that as a cornerstone, we understand that our living missionally before our children is the way they learn it. It's "caught" rather than "taught." No words you say will convince your kids that this is the way God wants them to live. Instead, a missional lifestyle will have to become such a part of you that it spills out into their lives. When they observe the contentment and fulfillment in you as you walk within the calling God has on your life, they are attracted to it.

But it can't be just your expressed belief system that makes your children want to be missional. So much theology has been bantered about concerning James 2 and the balance of faith and works in a believer's life. In the context of living your faith out in your home, this truth can be demonstrated more definitively than in any other arena.

What use is it, my brethren, if someone says he has faith but he has no works? Can that faith save him? If a brother or sister is without clothing and in need of daily food, and one of you says to them, 'Go in peace, be warmed and be filled,' and yet you do not give them

what is necessary for their body, what use is that? Even so faith, if it has no works, is dead, being by itself.
—James 2:14–17 (NASB)

While, in the big picture, there will always be discussions about the balance of faith and works in our lives, when we view it from what our children learn from us about God and His mission, what we do simply and vividly defines what we believe. What they see you do will authenticate how you are following Christ. Jesus gave His disciples an important directive about the value of teaching with our actions.

So now I am giving you a new commandment: Love each other. Just as I have loved you, you should love each other. Your love for one another will prove to the world that you are my disciples.
—John 13:34–35 (NLT)

That's the reason that we say this book is not really about parenting. It's about God's thoughts about you and me and the way we live our lives. It's about what He's planning for our kids. If we want our children to fulfill the mission that God has upon their lives, we are going to have to model it for them. Serving others, reaching out to them, and planting seeds of truth in their lives must become how our families operate. The living, breathing reality of our faith in action, the experience of God's calling being lived out in our lives, will teach our children what it means to be missional more than any words could ever convey. God has called each and every one of us to action. Get ready! Go!

THINK

▲ If I were to apply 1 Corinthians 13 to all my relationships, what might change about my demeanor at home? At work? In my neighborhood or apartment building?

▲ Thinking about the place where I live and work and all the people I interact with daily, what do I perceive might specifically be God's mission for my life right now?

▲ Do I ever isolate myself from being with other people? Why do I do that?

▲ Is my family's life so crowded with church activities that we never have an opportunity to be salt and light in our community? What can I do to change that?

▲ What have I done in the past week to offer help or friendship to another person that my family would be able to observe? If you have no answer, spend a moment in prayer, asking God to show you something practical that you can do. Now, go do it!

DO TRY THIS AT HOME!

❏ Instead of shoving tracts into their mailbox, invite your next-door neighbors over for coffee and a round of Monopoly. Listen to details about their families and jobs with interest. After they leave, have your whole family pray together for their needs and ask God to bless them.

❏ On trash collection day, carry the garbage cans to and from the house of an older couple on your block. After they've seen you do it a few times, if they haven't volunteered yet, enlist your middle-school or high-school-age kids to take on the task.

LIVE IT!

It was one of those crisp, sunny days that sometimes grace December in the Deep South, but Linda wasn't finding her usual joy in it.

As Mike lifted a duffle bag and a carry-on case out of the car, she struggled against a sick feeling in the pit of her stomach and tried to summon a calm smile for their 17-year-old daughter.

Andi caught her eye and broke into her best rendition of a song straight from one of Linda's old Peter, Paul, and Mary albums.

"All my bags are packed, I'm ready to go," she crooned, throwing an arm around her mother's shoulder. Moving on to the chorus of "New York, New York," Andi danced over to her dad in characteristic exuberance and continued to serenade him as they wheeled her luggage toward the airport check-in doors.

Following along behind them, Linda prayed for courage and peace to see her through the next hour, when they would put their talented, impetuous, joyful daughter on a plane for New York City. There she would use her considerable dramatic ability with a group doing sidewalk ministry on the streets in some of the roughest parts of that city.

Hearing Andi give a squeal, Linda looked up to see a couple from church, Cindy and Jim, coming toward them from the terminal, dragging bright pink suitcases. They were laughing with a young woman nearly invisible behind the bulging shopping bags loaded in her arms.

"Lauren!" Andi shouted, and ran to embrace the young woman who had been her church camp counselor and role model throughout her years in youth group. "I can't believe we ran into you! How was Ireland?"

Lauren, who was just returning from a year's mission to teenagers in Galway, shifted her bags and the two girls began an animated exchange. Cindy and Jim stood to the side with Mike and Linda, letting the girls have their moment to talk.

"So, is this it? Andi's headed for New York?" Jim asked Mike.

"Yep, today's the day," Mike said.

Putting a hand on Linda's shoulder, Cindy asked, "Are you doing OK?"

"I was so sure, but now that the day is here, I'm finding it really hard to let her go," Linda admitted. "How in the world did you and Jim do it?"

"It wasn't always easy," Cindy said, "especially when the fighting started in Afghanistan, and things were so unstable. When Lauren first told us about the chance to go to Ireland, my first thought was about what I had seen in the news about Belfast. My first question was, 'Are they still shooting there?'"

"That's it!" Linda said. "It's not like she's going to be at a church or on a college campus. I think about the streets, and my mind is filled with a million 'What ifs.'"

"I think that will always be something we have to contend with," Cindy said. "It's just a natural parental instinct. But when I looked back over the process, I realized that God had been working this into Lauren's life for a long time, and I found that I could trust Him."

With a glance at the girls still deep in conversation, she continued.

"Lauren went to Ireland first on a short-term mission. I thought at the time that her first motivation was not so much spiritual as it was the adventure. But on that trip, God showed her what she really needed to do," Cindy said. "There was this rough inner-city kid they had been working with for a long time, and Lauren led him to the Lord.

"It seems like God revealed His will to her, not through bolts of lightning, but from seeds He had planted all along. When she was invited to apply for the long-term ministry position, we questioned her about her motives," Cindy continued. "She told us she kept thinking about a line from a Psalty music tape, *Salvation Celebration* that she listened to when she was little. It said God had a destiny, a plan, and a purpose for her life. She said, 'If I don't apply, I'll never know if it's my destiny.'"

As the dads had become focused on their wives' conversation, Jim spoke up.

"Logically, it was a great time for her to do it. She had finished college, and she was single, with no obligations," he said. "We encouraged it, even though it was a stretch for us to believe for her finances.

"There were also reasons we could have killed the idea," Jim said. "Cindy and I were saving and planning for going to New Guinea on a medical mission ourselves, and the money wasn't there for both."

"And I thought it didn't fit in well with her education, her degree in public relations," Cindy added. "But then, I saw that Lauren is a people person, who loves kids and connects with them, and the mission in Galway, running the coffeehouse outreach to high school kids, would utilize those gifts. She had already been doing that at the summer camp where she worked."

"In the end," Jim said, "I just came to the place where I had to tell the Lord, 'She's yours. I have to give her up.' And then our job became just to keep her constantly in our prayers."

"And I'll tell you, she had plenty of struggles once she was there," Cindy said. "That kept us on our knees! The coffeehouse was in a rough part of town, surrounded by bars overlooking the canal, and she was living alone in rooms above the shop. As she dealt with her uneasiness and loneliness, we did, too."

"But God has been faithful, and used her in so many ways there, and while we've seen her grow, we've grown in our faith too," Jim said. "But I know today is a huge challenge for you both," he said, looking over at the girls.

"This didn't just come out of the blue for us with Andi either," Mike said. "In her first year of youth group, in sixth grade, a group spoke to the kids about missions trips they were doing around the world. Andi immediately felt that she was supposed to be a part of some mission."

"When she came home that night, there was an excitement about her that we'd never seen before," Linda said. "She was ready to pack her bags and leave the next day, if it were possible, to take the gospel to some other place."

"Linda and I were glad that the Lord had clearly spoken to her, but we weren't quite ready to send an 11-year-old little girl to some remote part of the world," Mike said, as the other three parents nodded in agreement.

"So years went by," Linda said, "and we would hear her heart over and over again, about how she wanted to go to Japan, Ireland, London, India—anywhere she heard that there were children needing to hear the gospel. Although she was maturing well, we were still not sure that we had heard from the Lord about this. Then in high school she discovered drama and became passionate about musical theatre, so naturally her interests grew to include New York City and Broadway. But she never lost the desire that the Lord had sparked in her heart six years earlier.

"One day a bulletin came in the mail from the same group, outlining future missions trips. Lo and behold," Linda said, "there was a trip to New York City that involved ministry to children and doing street evangelism using drama. Andi was sure that this trip was the opportunity for her finally to fulfill what the Lord had called her to do. When she approached us with this, we were immediately in agreement that this was the time and place for which God had called her."

Mike chuckled. "You know, it is amazing how it worked out, because Linda and I both knew and agreed instantly, which is somewhat a rarity in our house. Because of our different personalities, usually one of us is more analytical about such big decisions, so there is a lot of 'dialogue' that needs to happen before an agreement is made. But we knew this was from the Lord because both of us felt an emphatic yes in our spirits."

"Mike and I let her go through with the application because we saw how passionate Andi was about it," Linda said. "There was never any doubt in our minds that she was being obedient to the Lord. It's scary to think that my innocent, naïve 18-year-old daughter will be on the filthiest, most dangerous streets of the largest city in our country without parental protection or familiar neighbors, and without any safe, cuddly home to come back to at day's end," she said. "But in my heart I know God is empowering her to go. If she's not afraid, then I know that she has to go, because there are so many of us who would be afraid of ministering in that kind of place, with so many dangers."

"The Bible says that we are each one different parts of the body, not all arms or all heads," Mike added. "So if God is building Andi as an elbow, who am I to stop the function of His body? If we, out of fear, didn't let her go, then how could God accomplish what He purposed for her life or the lives of those she was ministering to? I don't want to stand before the Lord one day and be sorry that I stopped the flow because I was afraid or did not trust God with my daughter's life."

"It's hard to let her go," Linda said, "but like you guys, we know that if God called her, then He will protect her. Wherever God leads our girls and whatever He calls them to do, I know we must trust Him."

The girls joined their parents, Andi checking the time on her cell phone.

"Hey, I know you've got to get in there and check bags," Jim said, "but let me say a prayer before you go."

The six of them huddled up and Jim, with feeling born of experience, prayed, "Father, give us all the peace of knowing that You are a sovereign God and in Your loving hands we can trust. Amen."

With quick hugs, the group broke up, Andi and her dad picking up the pace as they headed to baggage check-in. Once again, Linda followed a few steps behind, but this time the feeling in her stomach was excitement for her daughter's adventure in faith.

CHAPTER 4

Publicans, Sinners, and That Guy Next Door

For I have not come to call the righteous, but sinners.
—Matthew 9:13 (NIV)

For God so loved the world. . . .
—John 3:16 (KJV)

Go ahead and finish it yourself. Even if you didn't grow up in Sunday School, you're certainly very familiar with this verse. John 3:16 contains the essence of God's story, and how it's linked to our story by the ultimate sacrifice. God demonstrated the nature and extent of His love when He offered His Son, Jesus, to die on a cross. And, Jesus willingly accepted His fate, even though, because of who He is, He could have been delivered from the suffering. Our focus is generally on the sacrificial act itself, as we try to comprehend love of such magnitude. The more we think about it, the more questions we have. Why did it have to happen like that? How could Jesus deliberately accept the anguish and give up His life?

The answer to all our questions is really very simple—"For God so loved the world." But that only introduces the most puzzling question of all: What's so special about the world? It's not the planet that He loves so much. It's people—all people, everywhere. He loves the people of every race, in every nation. He loves all people, no matter what they look like, no matter what their personality is. He loves smart people and slow people, the beautiful ones and the plain ones, heroes and villains. And He loves the unlovable—the irritating neighbor, the uncivilized tribesman, the dangerous criminal, the smelly homeless person, and even the ruthless despot. His love is lavish and limitless.

When we consider the extent of God's love and that it's directed toward each individual in the entire world, we're thankful and we're humbled, but we still find it difficult to fully understand. Our own best efforts at love are clouded by limitations, expectations, and self-interest. So, when we examine how we love compared to how God loves, the temptation is just to throw our hands up and declare that it's useless to try. Except, we're not given a pass to do that.

> *Jesus replied, "'You must love the Lord your God with all your heart, all your soul, and all your mind.' This is the first and greatest commandment. A second is equally important: 'Love your neighbor as yourself.'"*
> —Matthew 22:37–39 (NLT)

Loving people is not simply an attribute of a missional lifestyle. Jesus said that it was a requirement for all believers, equal in importance to our active and unreserved love for God. Jesus emphasized the necessity of loving people because He knew His Father's heart. He knew that God had made each person in His own image, created uniquely, with a plan and purpose in mind.

As parents, when we develop a Christlike love for people, it is contagious in our home. However, modeling to our children a love for people must be authentic on our part. Our actions must line up with our words in one united effort. We can't simply talk a good game, giving lip service to our care for people. And, in the same manner, what we say about loving people points out to our children the subtleties of serving. Considerate conversation about others and observable service to them establish a people-focused missional lifestyle in your home.

However, honestly loving people may be the most difficult challenge we have as believers because today's culture, with its me-first attitudes, has robbed us of the knowledge of what an authentic love for others looks like. We need to realign our perspective with how

Jesus loved people in order for our family to embrace those honest expressions of love and service.

Jesus knew people. One of the most disturbing trends in the church in recent years has been a foxhole mentality that some have seized in order to protect themselves from ungodly cultural influences. They have too often sought to insulate themselves within "all things Christian" at the expense of influencing their world through their involvement.

It's interesting that most people in Jesus' community didn't refer to Him as Messiah, Rabbi, or any other religious title. They called Him "the carpenter" (Mark 6:3). Carpenters were important people in Jesus' day because their skills were used in a much wider scope than just building dwellings. They crafted furniture, doors and windows, crates and chests, yokes and plows for farming, and other types of customized tools. Virtually everyone in the community had connections with the carpenter. Jesus worked alongside people every day. In fact, He was so familiar to them, that some of them had a difficult time viewing Him as Messiah.

> Jesus interacted with all types of people.

Even after He began His ministry, Jesus interacted with all types of people, talked with them, laughed with them, cried with them and loved them. The Pharisees, the religious aristocracy of the day, hated Jesus because He loved the "wrong" people. He had the audacity to dine with sinners and the despised tax collectors, touch lepers' diseased skin and share stories with prostitutes. His closest friends were fishermen, and the most obvious thing about them is that they smelled terrible.

To understand what being missional is all about, our children need to know people the way Jesus knew them. They need to understand that not all people believe what their family believes or live the way they live. Our kids need to realize that God has called them, too, to reflect Christ to their world. This doesn't mean that we simply let them loose to navigate the culture on their own. But, as parents, we can create opportunities where our children can see our families loving people and touching lives. Invite the next-door neighbors over, or be bold and throw a block party. Encourage your kids to invite friends to your house, and show them how to make those friends feel welcome. Have snacks and smiles ready. Show your family how to be friendly!

Jesus was authentic. If you were God here on earth, how would you act? Most of us would probably determine that some sort of royal mannerisms would be in order. It would call for a self-righteous, sanctimonious attitude, wouldn't it? And certainly, an occasional demonstration of power and wrath would remind everyone who was in charge. Lightning bolts would be especially impressive. It's interesting that we never see any of that kind of behavior in Jesus. We never see people too fearful of Jesus to speak to Him. They didn't feel He was too important to be bothered by them or too holy to be available to them. People had conversations with Him, and they invited Him to dinner and to parties. We know of at least one occasion when He even invited Himself to someone's house. People reached out to Jesus and pressed in close to Him. They wanted to touch Him.

Jesus was so approachable because He was real. Nobody ever seemed uncomfortable around Him except for hypocrites. He was honest about His opinions, yet because He loved people so much, they weren't offended. Jesus never played the holier-than-thou card. He was completely authentic, with no pretenses, and everyone felt at ease with that.

Missional people are real, just like Jesus. And, genuineness produces an aroma that people can easily sniff out. Children are especially astute at identifying it, as if they were fitted with some sort of truth-detecting radar. As we proceed on our journey with Christ, our children will observe the reality of our walk. And they take notes. While our tendencies are to put a lid on our struggles and present a good face, kids can learn from an authentic display of the grace and beauty of Jesus shining through us in the midst of troubles. Rehearsed niceties spoken about people won't have the effect on your family that the visual of real and practical service would have. Authentic love is dangerous. It's not easy for us to be exposed like that. But those who know you best and love you most will respond to real expressions of love, and it becomes wildly contagious.

So much of today's Christian ministry is displayed in the public arena, under the scrutiny of a culture that constantly judges its merit and its integrity. The criticism has often been harsh, sometimes unfairly so, but at other times, we've deserved the slams that we received.

Jesus never sought the spotlight. In fact, at various times in the Gospels' accounts of His life, He told those around Him that He didn't want to be a spectacle. In the midst of miracles that He performed, life-changing truth that He declared, and a revolutionary message of love and grace that He delivered, He made it known that the focus was not to be upon Him.

> Then a leper appeared and went to his knees before Jesus, praying, "Master, if you want to, you can heal my body." Jesus reached out and touched him, saying, "I want to. Be clean." Then and there, all signs of the leprosy were gone. Jesus said, "Don't talk about this all over town. Just quietly present your healed body to the priest, along with the appropriate expressions of thanks to God. Your cleansed and grateful life, not your words, will bear witness to what I have done."
> —Matthew 8:2–4 (*The Message*)

Human nature craves attention. In fact, we love attention so much that often the next best thing to receiving attention ourselves is lavishing it on someone else. We enjoy being flattered, and we also enjoy flattering others. Flattery, either coming or going, feels good. And that's the root of the problem. It's a whole lot like what we see in today's music culture, among the superstars. While the performer receives the obvious attention from fans, the media, and others who want a piece of them, there is also an underground entourage who gets their own rush by just reacting to every whim of the superstars.

Because that whole attention-grabbing scene is so self-fulfilling, it can even exist in the midst of serving and loving others. We can find ourselves doing it because it makes us feel good or just so we can be around the rarified air where everyone is patting each other on the back (because "we're all such good people").

Loving people has nothing to do with us, but everything to do with the people we love. That is the message that our children should hear from us loudly and clearly, although modeled for them quietly and subtly.

So, if our ministry to others is supposed to be so inconspicuous, how can our families see it? Real love starts right at home. They will see it when moms and dads are completely devoted to each other and when parents put their kids' needs above their own agendas. You don't have to point out that kind of love. It never needs a spotlight to be noticed or a loudspeaker to be heard.

What does our love really look like? When we minister to others, what exactly is our motivation? Love can't come dressed in a Superman costume, with the intent of rescuing poor misguided souls. Our goal is not to convince people. The Holy Spirit does that. Our ministry is not to save people. That's Jesus' responsibility. Our job doesn't include changing people. God handles that. The calling that God has for us is to befriend, bump into, run across, and experience the people He places in our lives, casually and every day. Our mission is to love people, honestly, selflessly, and limitlessly.

THINK

▲ In meditating on John 3:16–17, what are the characteristics of God's love that should be more evident in my life?

▲ As I consider Matthew 22:37–39, on a scale of one to ten, how well do I love God with all my heart, soul, and mind? In what areas do I need to improve? On that same scale, how unselfishly do I love my neighbors? How can I improve that?

▲ What specifically has my family observed of my unselfishgiving to other people?

▲ What adjustments can I make in my lifestyle that will enable me to rub shoulders with more people?

DO TRY THIS AT HOME!

❏ Be active in your PTA and neighborhood association. Through those organizations, encourage whole families in your neighborhood to get together to socialize and take on projects.

❏ Bring your family to your neighborhood school, garbage bags in hand, and pick up trash on the campus. Tell your kids to pray silently for the administration, teachers and students while you're at work there.

❏ Here's a great way to get good exercise while you minister to your neighbors! Gather your family together after dinner and take a walk through your neighborhood. Tell your children to observe people and situations all around them there. Be sure to speak to everyone you encounter en route. When you get home, talk about needs that you saw that you want to be in prayer about or areas you saw where you might lend a helping hand.

❏ Encourage your family's creativity. Brainstorm ways you can serve people around you, reminding everyone to be aware of opportunities where they can serve people, even in small, quiet ways. And remember, they learn this lesson more easily when they see you practicing what you preach!

░░ ░░ ░░ LIVE IT! ░░ ░░ ░░

Nine-year-old Jason Russell stood peering through the glass case at an array of video cameras, his right hand in his jeans pocket, touching the wallet that finally held enough money to fund his long-awaited purchase.

"I want that one," he told the clerk after long deliberation, proudly handing over the cash he had earned himself. Ecstatically clutching his new camera, he headed with his mom to the car, already planning the stories he would be able to tell.

His mother, Sheryl, had already noticed some unique qualities in her son's life.

"Jason had a tender heart from a young age. He was creative and was always willing to put on a play with his brother and sisters. He grew up in a theater family and therefore had opportunities to develop his God-given talent," she explained.

Jason's father taught high school drama, and Sheryl and her husband saw to it that he was given acting, singing and dancing lessons. He also had plenty of time to play outside and be creative, instead of spending time in front of a television set.

"When Jason was in fourth grade, he had an opportunity to be in a local play that paid him. With that money, he bought his first video camera," Sheryl said. "When friends would come over, they would film a story. Jason was the director and got lots of friends to go along with his ideas," she said.

"God got hold of Jason's heart at a young age. We had Backyard Bible Club at our home, and one day he was sitting in his little red wagon with his children's Bible telling a neighbor friend about Jesus. He was a storyteller.

"I think his Dad and brother helped to shape his worldview. There were always lively discussions around the dinner table. They would challenge each other's opinions. He was also involved in his youth group at church and had opportunities to serve others," Jason's mom continued.

It didn't seem like long before his brand-new degree from the University of Southern California's film school occupied a place of honor over Jason's computer desk. His friends, Bobby Bailey and Laren Poole, looked over his shoulder searching eBay for exactly the right camera for their long-awaited film-making adventure in Africa, little imagining what God had in mind for them there. Though the idea for the trip was open-ended, the seeds had been planted several years earlier.

"His first trip to Africa was with a missions group. It was organized and had adults in charge," Sheryl said. "After he graduated from USC Film School, he wanted to document the persecution in Southern Sudan. I felt like he was flying to an unknown place, getting off a plane and asking, 'Where are the guns, I want to document the story.' I suggested he make some contacts in Africa before he headed out. He spent months making contacts with people in Africa. When he left, he had a list of people who were willing to meet him and work with him.

"The day we put him on a plane at LAX, President Bush was asking all Americans to stay home because we had declared war on Iraq. What kind of a mother was I to let my son go to a war-torn country where he didn't know anyone? I went to India when I was 21, so I knew the feeling of going to a foreign country, getting off a plane and not knowing a single person. When Jason went in 2003, communication was limited. I couldn't call him every day and email was difficult to send. The unknown is always fearful. I remember going a week without hearing a word, and the only number I had, no one was answering. Thoughts went through my mind that possibly something had happened to him. And how would I know? I can say that in the midst of my deepest fears, God was giving a peace that only He can give," she recounted.

"At the time, I didn't realize the dangerous aspect of the story they found in Northern Uganda. I remember the day he called and asked me to extend their plane tickets because they had 'found their story.' I have since had the opportunity to travel to Northern

Uganda to see first hand the work that is taking place," she said.

It was when the three young men found themselves stranded in Northern Uganda that the story took what they call a "divine turn." They discovered children being kidnapped nightly from their homes and forced to fight as child soldiers, a horrible situation about which the rest of the world seemed unaware.

The film they brought back, entitled *Invisible Children: Rough Cut*, was originally shown to friends and family in 2004. But it soon found showings in high schools and churches, eventually making its way to Capitol Hill and CNN.

Because the story the movie tells is so compelling, the Invisible Children movement was born, and citizens and governments across the globe have taken up the cause of saving children from a horror that has existed for over 20 years.

Looking back at her years of parenting, Sheryl says, "I feel all four of our children have done great things in the areas God has gifted them. They all had the same parenting, and yet they are four unique individuals. I believe God has gifted us with different talents and strengths. What we do with them is what will make the difference."

What would she say to other parents whose kids have big, and perhaps dangerous, dreams?

"As a parent, there is no greater joy than to see your children desiring to use their gifts and talents to fulfill the second greatest commandment, 'Love your neighbor as yourself.' I would tell them to let go and let God."

NOTE: For more details about Jason's experience and information on the Invisible Children, go to the Web site: InvisibleChildren.com.

CHAPTER 5

Eye Chart and #2 Pencil Not Needed

"And the King will say, 'I tell you the truth, when you did it to one of the least of these my brothers and sisters, you were doing it to me!'"
—Matthew 25:40 (NLT)

ow, it's time to take a test." If that statement causes you to break out in a cold sweat, flashing back to your days in school, just relax. You're not actually going to need that trusty #2 pencil for this, because this exam is just one question. But, even though it's just a simple multiple choice, the answer may reveal more about you than you ever wanted to know. Attention, please, here's the question:

Imagine you're walking through a seamy urban area of a major American city. Any American city will do. On the sidewalk lying up against the door of an abandoned old store, and right in your path, is a homeless man, obviously intoxicated and passed out. He's urinated on himself, and it's probably been weeks since he's bathed. What are you feeling? Check one:

- a. Disgusted. I think I might throw up.
- b. Frightened. I'm going to get to the other side of the street as soon as possible.

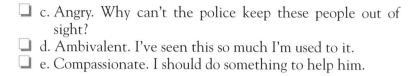

□ c. Angry. Why can't the police keep these people out of sight?

□ d. Ambivalent. I've seen this so much I'm used to it.

□ e. Compassionate. I should do something to help him.

You know that probably you should have answered E, but the fact is almost all of us, if we're honest, would choose A, B, C, or D. We know that Jesus was compassionate, and we understand that He's our pattern for how to love people. He even told a story very similar to this scenario, just so we captured the concept of loving people the way He wanted us to love them. It was about a Samaritan who really was compassionate and made the effort to rescue someone in trouble while other "religious" people did, honestly, what we would have probably done. They ignored the man who was in trouble, possibly because they were just too busy, or they simply didn't want to get involved.

Often, when it comes to loving people Jesus' way, we fail miserably. So the big question is, why can't we get it right? That's our struggle. We know there's a way that we're supposed to treat people, and we know that we have an obligation to help someone who is in need and to point them to Christ, but when it comes time for action we just fail to do what we know we should do. We know that this is something, too, that our children learn from watching us. We want our children to see us modeling compassion and love toward others, but we can think of a thousand reasons why it's not safe, practical or timely. We really know what we should do, but somehow there is a disconnect between our brain, our heart and our actions. Can you identify with the frustration Paul felt when he wrote about this?

I can will it, but I can't do it. I decide to do good, but I don't really do it; I decide not to do bad, but then I do it anyway. My decisions, such as they are, don't result in actions. Something has gone wrong deep within me and gets the better of me every time. It happens so regularly that it's predictable.
—Romans 7:19–21 (*The Message*)

Despite the discouragement that our failures have brought us, how do we begin seeing people the way Jesus saw them? Just as our kids learn the lessons of compassion from observing our hearts in action, Jesus modeled His love of people for His disciples. When He called Simon Peter and Andrew to their mission to be fishers of men, He

Let It Shine!

didn't provide them a prescription about how to love people. There was not a set of instructions or a process of exercises that they had to go through. He just simply said to them, "Follow me." He wanted Simon Peter and Andrew to come along and observe Him, because there was something in the way that He viewed people that would reveal to them the key to being compassionate.

So, let's do just that. Let's go on a little journey with Jesus. And, on the way, we'll be taking a crash course in Compassion 101, observing how He loved others. From it, we'll learn what it takes to demonstrate Christlike compassion, so that we can inspire our children to have a heart that loves others. Let's examine a day from Jesus' life, as chronicled in Matthew 9, and follow Him, as He invited Simon Peter and Andrew to do. We'll join Him on a boat to begin the trip, as He crosses the Sea of Galilee, into Capernaum, where He was living at the time.

> *Getting into a boat, Jesus crossed over the sea and came to His own city. And they brought to Him a paralytic lying on a bed. Seeing their faith, Jesus said to the paralytic, "Take courage, son; your sins are forgiven."... Then He said to the paralytic, "Get up, pick up your bed and go home." And he got up and went home. But when the crowds saw this, they were awestruck, and glorified God, who had given such authority to men.*
> —Matthew 9:1–2, 6–8 (NASB)

This is a familiar story that we have read in some of the other Gospels as well. Do you recall the men who climbed up on the top of the house where Jesus was speaking, removed the roofing tiles and lowered their paralyzed friend on a stretcher into the room where Jesus was? This is Matthew's brief account of that event.

Jesus observed the extent to which the man and his friends would go to bring the paralyzed man to Jesus. Their great effort and faith touched Him. He understood that for them to go to such lengths, they most certainly were desperate for healing. But Jesus' empathy with the man's situation exposed another need that was equally pressing. Imagine the helplessness that would accompany being paralyzed. The man most certainly felt that he was a burden on his friends who had to carry him wherever he wanted to go. He was deprived of his dignity and depended completely on the charity of others even to exist. Because of his plight, he was a prime candidate for bitterness and resentment to eat away at his soul. Knowing all this, Jesus not only spoke words of healing to the man's body, He ministered courage to his spirit and forgiveness to his soul.

> *And some of the scribes said to themselves, "This fellow blasphemes." And Jesus knowing their thoughts said, "Why are you thinking evil in your hearts? Which is easier, to say, 'Your sins are forgiven,' or to say, 'Get up, and walk'? But so that you may know that the Son of Man has authority on earth to forgive sins"—then He said to the paralytic, "Get up, pick up your bed and go home."*
> —Matthew 9:3–6 (NASB)

The religious leaders stood in judgment of everything that Jesus said and did. They whispered their disparaging remarks about Him behind His back. Their legalistic posturing was all about them and had nothing at all to do with responding to people's needs. The scribes needed to compartmentalize Jesus to control Him, so they went to great lengths to question the legitimacy of His actions and His approach. But Jesus wanted them to know that His mission was about people and wholeness for their entire being.

> *As Jesus went on from there, He saw a man called Matthew, sitting in the tax collector's booth; and He said to him, "Follow Me!" And he got up and followed Him. Then it happened that as Jesus was reclining at the table in the house, behold, many tax collectors and sinners came and were dining with Jesus and His disciples.*
> —Matthew 9:9–10 (NASB)

Jesus wasn't controlled by propriety or the political correctness of His culture. He responded to people with compassion for their needs and for their situations. He didn't need the approval of others to validate His actions. He understood that even vicious and offensive people were acting out as the result of much deeper hurts. What would be the most needful thing for Matthew, a tax collector who was hated and reviled by every aspect of society? He was starved for acceptance and the fellowship of sharing a meal with someone—anyone who would accept him. He was isolated and most likely lonely and hurting. Jesus wasn't turned off by the hateful and dishonest dealings of a man who had forgotten what it felt like to have friends. Apparently Jesus' invitation was so genuine that even someone as jaded as Matthew felt completely comfortable walking away from what he was doing and joining Jesus for dinner. Not only Matthew, but others who had the same reviled station in life, saw the love that Jesus demonstrated and wanted to soak it up along with Matthew.

> *When the Pharisees saw this, they said to His disciples, "Why is your Teacher eating with the tax collectors and sinners?" But when Jesus heard this, He said, "It is not those who are healthy who need a physician, but those who are sick. But go and learn what this means: 'I desire compassion and not sacrifice,' for I did not come to call the righteous, but sinners."*
> —Matthew 9:11–13 (NASB)

Once again, Jesus was indirectly confronted by the pseudreligious who were skulking around the perimeters, gossiping, and trying to stir up trouble. They were inferring that if He were really a man of God, He would desire their pious company more than that of the social outcasts He was eating with. When He heard them, He challenged their self-righteousness with a logical response that cut to the core of their own sin. If they were truly righteous, they didn't need His healing. He would be wasting His time spending it with people like them—people who had it all together. He justified His ministry by confronting the Pharisees with their own law: "I desire compassion and not sacrifice." The disreputable characters Jesus was dining with came to Him with no pretenses. They knew that their souls were sick, and they eagerly responded to the truth that He was sharing with them.

> Jesus provided inspiration, encouraging them to find joy in all they did.

> *A little later John's followers approached, asking, "Why is it that we and the Pharisees rigorously discipline body and spirit by fasting, but your followers don't?" Jesus told them, "When you're celebrating a wedding, you don't skimp on the cake and wine. You feast. Later you may need to pull in your belt, but not now. No one throws cold water on a friendly bonfire. This is Kingdom Come!" He went on, "No one cuts up a fine silk scarf to patch old work clothes; you want fabrics that match. And you don't put your wine in cracked bottles."*
> —Matthew 9:14–17 (*The Message*)

Apparently the Pharisees succeeded with their backbiting. They had concluded that if they couldn't win the debate with Jesus directly, they would exploit those that were a bit closer to Him and more accepted by those who were around Him. John's followers took up the legalistic torch, accusing Jesus and His disciples of not really being as righteous as they were, because they didn't see Him fasting as often as they fasted. Though John's disciples seemed to be susceptible to the same prideful attitudes demonstrated by the Pharisees, Jesus saw that the root of the problem was quite different. John had been imprisoned for some time, and unable to bring a fresh word and new inspiration to those believers who followed him and learned from him. They had dug themselves into a rut. They were frozen in time.

Did you ever see that classic movie *Groundhog Day*? The main character was stuck at February 2, and that day replayed repeatedly. John's followers were faced with a similar nightmare because they expected everything to happen the same way it had always happened. They weren't experiencing the joy of a dynamic walk with the Son of God, the new wine of His Word. So Jesus provided words of inspiration, encouraging them to find joy in all that they did.

> *While He was saying these things to them, a synagogue official came and bowed down before Him, and said, "My daughter has just died; but come and lay Your hand on her, and she will live." Jesus got up and began to follow him, and so did His disciples.... When Jesus came into the official's house, and saw the flute-players and the crowd in noisy disorder, He said, "Leave; for the girl has not died, but is asleep." And they began laughing at Him. But when the crowd had been sent out, He entered and took her by the hand, and the girl got up. This news spread throughout all that land.*
> —Matthew 9:18–19, 23–26 (NASB)

Desperate people seek desperate solutions. While so many of the religious leaders were trying to trap Jesus in some heresy, He could have felt justified in just ignoring Jairus (Mark tells us his name), the supervisor of all the activities at the local synagogue. That would have been a natural reaction to religious leaders who were so bent on his destruction. But Jesus' heart of compassion responded to Jairus. In his important role at the synagogue, he presided over many ceremonies of burial, but now death and its finality had personally touched his family. When it was his own daughter who had died, Jairus knew that there was nobody else who could possibly help now but Jesus. With all the desperation that cries from the heart of a parent who has lost a child, Jairus told Jesus he knew that if He would just touch his daughter, she would live again. Jesus felt this man's desperation and understood his grief. He went to Jairus' home, stopped the funeral procession, and raised the little girl from the dead.

> *And a woman who had been suffering from a hemorrhage for twelve years, came up behind Him and touched the fringe of His cloak; for she was saying to herself, "If I only touch His garment, I will get well." But Jesus turning and seeing her said, "Daughter, take courage; your faith has made you well." At once the woman was made well.*
> —Matthew 9:20–22 (NASB)

In the midst of a crowd of people pressing against Him and trying to get as close as possible, Jesus sensed something different. Although she was weak from a terrible disease, a little woman was determined to touch Him. She decided if she could get close enough to just touch His robe, she would be healed. When she was able to press in closer and her hand brushed against His garment, Jesus immediately asked, "Who touched me?" It could have been anyone in the crowd that was pressing in all around Him. But He was so in touch with these people and so compassionate toward those in need that He realized someone there had especially sought Him out. He looked into her eyes and declared that her faith had made her well.

> *As Jesus went on from there, two blind men followed Him, crying out, "Have mercy on us, Son of David!" When He entered the house, the blind men came up to Him, and Jesus said to them, "Do you believe that I am able to do this?" They said to Him, "Yes, Lord." Then He touched their eyes, saying, "It shall be done to you according to your faith." And their eyes were opened. And Jesus sternly warned them: "See that no one knows about this!" But they went out and spread the news about Him throughout all that land.*
> —Matthew 9:27–31 (NASB)

Don't you find it interesting that before Jesus healed the two blind men, He asked them a question? On the surface, their need seemed pretty obvious. They were calling out to Jesus, asking Him to heal their blindness. He reached down much further though and inquired about the measure of their faith. Jesus' perception was that the condition of their soul and spirit was of primary importance. His priority was to hear an expression of their belief, and when they didn't hesitate, responding with a resounding "Yes!", Jesus healed them. From His point of view, as important as their physical healing was, the condition of their souls was more important.

There was another interesting aspect of this encounter. After he healed the men, Jesus specifically told them not to talk about it. Jesus' mission was not about drawing attention to Himself or even His ministry. We could reasonably defend the notion that it was important to spread the word to as many people as possible, but drawing a crowd was not Jesus' objective. Individuals were His focus. He looked into a person's eyes but could read what was inside the heart. He saw the *person*, not as a problem and not even an opportunity.

> *As they were going out, a mute, demon-possessed man was brought to Him. After the demon was cast out, the mute man spoke; and the crowds were amazed, and were saying, "Nothing like this has ever been seen in Israel."*
> —Matthew 9:32–33 (NASB)

Jesus was confident. He trusted completely in God's work through Him. In the midst of difficult situations that could have been intimidating and even frightening, Jesus was secure in His mission because He knew that God had called Him. There was no spiritual battle that was so severe, no person whose life was so chaotic, no situation that was so formidable, but that Jesus knew that God's power was sufficient. Because he had that assurance, Jesus never fled from what He had to face.

> *Jesus went through all the towns and villages, teaching in their synagogues, preaching the good news of the kingdom and healing every disease and sickness. When he saw the crowds, he had compassion on them, because they were harassed and helpless, like sheep without a shepherd. Then he said to his disciples, "The harvest is plentiful but the workers are few. Ask the Lord of the harvest, therefore, to send out workers into his harvest field."*
> —Matthew 9:35–38 (NIV)

Jesus was intent about impacting His world, directing His whole being toward fulfilling that mission. But, most of all, He was mindful of people. His heart broke for them because He empathized with their plight. They were lost, fearful, hurting and confused, and even though their pain sometimes manifested itself in ridiculous behavior or hurtful attitudes, it didn't discourage Him from loving each one of them. Jesus saw the gravity of the situation. He understood that time was of the essence and wasted minutes were counterproductive. He urged all of us to join Him in the work that needs to be done.

Following Jesus and observing His interaction with people reveals some remarkable aspects of His heart. These attitudes provided the impetus for His mission and shaped His ministry. His perspective was reflective of the character of God, His Father. In Jesus' heart and through His eyes, we are able to discover the way to love people selflessly and wholeheartedly. There were three aspects of Jesus' point of view that were evident in His authentic love of people and His compassion for their circumstances:

> Why do people behave the way they do?

Jesus looked beyond the obvious and saw the real need. Why do people behave the way they do? Psychologists might condense it to its most basic elements—environment affects attitudes, attitudes affect habits, and habits affect behavior. Jesus' compassion toward people was predicated on the fact He knew that beyond a person's surface appearance and conduct, there existed needs and hurts that made them act the way they did. Jesus had compassion for people despite their actions and words. He understood that the healing that people need is for their whole person, body, soul and spirit.

Dietrich Bonhoeffer had Jesus' perspective toward the unseemly behavior that some people demonstrate. He wasn't just a casual observer of human nature. After Adolph Hitler and his Nazi party took over Germany, they systematically set out to crush all who challenged the power and principles they espoused and enacted. Bonhoeffer, a German pastor, rebelled and vehemently stood his ground against the dictator. As a result, he suffered severe, relentless persecution, imprisonment, and eventually death at the hands of the Nazis. He refused to back down, but he also refused to be bitter. "We must learn to regard people less in light of what they do or omit to do," Bonhoeffer said as he awaited execution in a Nazi prison, "and more in the light of what they suffer. The only profitable relationship to others—and especially to our weaker brethren—is one of love, and that means the will to hold fellowship with them. God himself did not despise humanity, but became man for men's sake."

Problems that people face are rarely one-dimensional. The reason for a person's unseemly behavior is almost always rooted deep inside. Responding to the whole person brings complete healing.

Jesus had a mission, but He didn't have an agenda. An agenda is, according to the dictionary, a predetermined list of things one has to do. That means that an agenda is focused on the doer, not on others. An agenda keeps score and views people as targets. A mission sees people, simply, as people.

Jesus responded to people rather than reacting to them. He didn't meet people and draw immediate conclusions from knee-jerk reactions. A reaction is a prejudiced, predetermined, thoughtless reflex. A response is a conscious, deliberate, premeditated action. If we react to the people that we come in contact with, our interaction is completely surface. Jesus responded to the desperate needs and impassioned cries that emanated from deep within those he encountered.

More than any other aspect of the missional lifestyle, authentic Christlike love for others is essential, and there is no other way for that to take hold in our family except for us to demonstrate it daily. Attitudes can't be kept hidden because they rise to the surface in times of anxiety or when we're caught off-guard. So, what Jesus modeled for us, we must make a part of who we are. Then who we really are becomes that pattern for who our kids become.

We first have to prayerfully seek that kind of heart. You might be amazed at the changes inside you when you begin to honestly and fervently ask God to allow you to see people the way He sees them.

But just asking, however sincerely, is probably not going to complete the transformation. We need to be conscious of our internally scripted reactions toward people and change them to intentional responses. God taught Samuel that lesson when He sent him to anoint the new king of Israel, one of Jesse's sons. Samuel approached the task, his head loaded with all the "king qualities" that he thought were necessary—good looks, physical strength, intelligence, and charisma. As all the young men were paraded before him, God interrupted Samuel with one crucial consideration.

> *The LORD does not look at the things man looks at. Man looks at the outward appearance, but the LORD looks at the heart.*
> —1 Samuel 16:7 (NIV)

Samuel had to rethink the way he saw people. Looking at a person's heart requires one step beyond our initial reactions. God wants us to ask ourselves questions about people. What's their motivation? What's behind their behavior? What exactly do they need?

As our authentic love for people is renewed, our practical response to their real needs becomes our mission. Then Christlike compassion is what our family observes and begins to learn. Our children's questions about those people in need are inevitable when they watch us reach out to others. When they see the fulfillment we experience in selflessly ministering to others, they begin to desire the same involvement. When they understand that people are simply people, all of them loved by God and part of His creation, they comprehend that God's blessing on your family requires something in response.

THINK

▲ What are some of the things that get in the way of our family reaching out to others?

▲ Thinking of your attempts at ministry and service, what things have you done as a mission? What might have been treated as an agenda?

▲ Consider the people that you and your family members encountered just this week. What was their real need? How could you have responded?

❏ OK, the barista at Starbuck's is sporting a Satanist pentagram on his T-shirt, and his arms are covered in snake tats. He has more piercings than you can count on all your fingers, and his hair and beard—well, they're just too much to even explain. Instead of frowning and shaking your head about how ridiculous you think he looks, how about smiling, asking him how is day is going and leaving him a nice tip?

❏ Most of the fast-food restaurants in your area offer gift certificates in as small a denomination as $1. If you're concerned about how a homeless person might spend cash that you give him, keep a supply of the gift certificates in your car and hand them out instead.

❏ Here's a spiritual experiment for you. Pray that you'll begin to see people as God sees them. Ask Him to give you a compassionate heart, one that's broken for the hurts and needs of others. You might be changed forever.

━━ ━━ ━━ LIVE IT! ━━ ━━ ━━

The oppressive summer heat beats down on the field where 80 men labor to impress the coaching staff with their skills and determination. The clatter of colliding shoulder pads and helmets mingles with the grunts and growls of intense competition to fill the empty stadium. Each athlete gathers every ounce of effort left within his weary body and uncoils it across the line of scrimmage to produce violent hits and deceptive movements that might allow them to continue their lifelong dream of playing professional football. Don't try to tell any of them that preseason training camp is meaningless.

Samkon Gado positions himself in the backfield, his powerful biceps taut, anticipating the handoff from the quarterback. At the snap, he lunges toward the line of scrimmage, and the football settles into his midsection. He darts and dances through the defense for precious yardage and then, suddenly, he is blindsided by a beefy linebacker. His knees ache, his ears are ringing, his head is throbbing, and he's dead tired. He would love just to stay down on the turf for a few moments and gather himself, but he knows that any sign of weakness will cause the coaches to question his value to the team. So he springs to his feet and readies himself to get hit once again.

"I've known for many years that God wanted me to be a missionary," Samkon said later. "I remember praying that He would send me somewhere that was very difficult, where the people I was around really needed to hear the gospel. I had no idea that God would answer my prayer by sending me to the National Football League."

Samkon had come a long way from his beginnings in many ways.

Nine-year-old Samkon was at the same time very sad and very excited. He was leaving his home in Funai, Nigeria, on his way to the United States, where he, his mother Grace, and the rest of his family would be reunited with his father, Jeremiah Gado. Jeremiah had been in Columbia, South Carolina, for a year, studying for his doctor of ministry degree and building support for his missions work of establishing churches and Bible schools throughout Nigeria and Ghana. The South Carolina church in which Jeremiah was involved in ministry now provided the opportunity for the entire Gado family to be together again.

After arriving in the United States, Samkon quickly became acclimated to the new culture. His outgoing personality soon won him friends, and his success in the classroom drew the attention of his teachers. It didn't take long for him to talk like an American and fit into the American way of life.

And then he discovered football. Back in Nigeria, he had heard some American missionary friends talking about this unusual sport, but all he knew about it when he got to the United States was that it was played with a very odd-shaped ball. Once he began to watch the game, observing the action and the strategy involved, his athlete's heart began to call him to participate.

The big hurdle was to convince his parents to let him play. Samkon and his older sister, Ruth, reasoned that the best way to plead his case was over the phone while their dad was in Africa on a missions trip. Jeremiah and Grace offered all the usual parental arguments about the violence of the sport, but when through tears Samkon kept begging, they reluctantly gave their permission.

His quickness and strength made him a natural at running back. Samkon excelled not only on the gridiron at Bin Lippen High School in Columbia, but he also lettered in track, soccer and basketball. He was named Athlete of the Year at Lippen and served as a captain on the football team.

Liberty University in Virginia recognized his potential as a running back and offered him a scholarship. Although Samkon only started two games there, his contributions were significant. His grit and power made him a threat near the goal line, and he amassed a team-leading 22 touchdowns during his career.

A nonstarter on the collegiate level usually has little opportunity to make it to the pros. But Samkon's athleticism and nose for the end zone made him legendary among NFL scouts, and soon their curiosity caused him to be the object of league chatter. Could he be the "sleeper," the Cinderella story that football teams always hope for? The Kansas City Chiefs took a chance and brought him into training camp in 2005, and Samkon impressed the staff there. But with superstars Priest Holmes and Larry Johnson ahead of him on the depth charts, he became expendable.

A few weeks later, when the Green Bay Packers' backfield became depleted by injuries, they were eager to give Samkon a closer look. Immediately, he made an impact and before the year ended, he had set most of the Packers' rookie rushing records.

Several years later, after stints in Houston, Miami, and St. Louis, Samkon continues his pro football career. As each opportunity arises, he obediently follows the path that God lays out before him, not always understanding, but always walking confidently.

If immigrating to the United States and becoming a pro football player was the culmination of all of Samkon's life goals, it would indeed be a remarkable story. Despite the ups and downs of injuries, trades and rosters changes, many people would give anything to be in Samkon's place. For them, the glory, the crowds and the money far outweigh the uncertainties of a career in professional sports. But Samkon Gado is about much more than football. While many of his peers in the locker room have achieved all they've ever dreamed of by their mid-20s, Samkon recognizes that this opportunity is simply a platform for a greater calling that has burned within him for many years.

When Samkon was 12 years old he began to understand that, apart from the strong faith of his parents and their influence in his life, he needed to experience God himself, and he asked Christ into his life. "From that very moment, God placed a desire in my heart for missions," he said. "I fought it and rationalized against it for eight years because it's a hard life, and I didn't want it."

Instead, Samkon's career choice was to become a doctor. "When I was a sophomore in high school, I took biology, and I really liked it," he said. "Something clicked, and I became interested in becoming a doctor." He majored in premed at Liberty, with the intent of continuing on to medical school, but football and one specific Wednesday evening church service during his second year in college began to redefine his plans.

"The service really wasn't even focused on missions," Samkon said. "But God spoke clearly to me that evening that He wanted me to surrender all my decision-making privileges to Him. I told Him, 'I surrender! Whatever you have for me is what I'll do.'"

He rushed back to the campus to phone his parents and tell them the news. "I told them that I knew for sure that God was preparing me for cross-cultural missions, and that I was to serve in Africa," Samkon said. "My mother hesitated at first. She wouldn't give me her blessing until she sought God about it. And He spoke to her, 'You have to let him go.'"

Grace Gado knew firsthand the difficult life of a missionary. She and her husband, Jeremiah, had dedicated their lives to serving the people of Africa. Although, for her, it had been rewarding and fulfilling, her hopes had been that her children's callings would not be as arduous. When Samkon expressed a desire to become a doctor, she had envisioned for him a successful private practice in their adopted home in the United States. Instead, he announced his plans to return to Nigeria. Suddenly her motherly instincts responded with the desire to protect her son. But she understood that unless he followed God, Samkon would never know the joys that she and Jeremiah had known in fulfilling His call.

Jeremiah's father and mother, Samkon's grandparents, became Christians through the ministry of missionaries more than 60 years ago. Following their conversion, they dedicated their lives to bringing Christ to people throughout Nigeria. Jeremiah had seen the disappointments and hardships of his parents' ministry as well as the victories. Still, he was not deterred from following God's plan for his life. His ministry in the United States and Africa has been rich and vibrant. Jeremiah and Grace have four daughters in addition to Samkon, all of whom actively serve God and are intent upon following His mission for their lives. Their oldest daughter, Ruth, is involved in urban ministry in north Philadelphia, serving the practical needs of the underprivileged there, and planting a church in the inner-city community.

"My parents are the greatest two people in the world," Samkon said. "They're flawed, like all of us, but they've done their job as parents—they've pointed us to the Cross. From the moment we were born, they taught each of us about Jesus and righteousness and the kingdom of God."

Looking back through his life, Samkon has gained some valuable insight concerning the course that it has taken. "I've learned that God places these desires in my heart—for football, for medicine, for missions—and it's for His purposes, not mine. I understand that wanting these things is not selfish as long as they're in their rightful place." With that prevailing priority, Samkon plans on weighing each opportunity that God places before him, moving prayerfully as God directs him.

He has passed the Medical College Admission Test (MCAT), but while he is still playing professional football, he will continue to retake it to increase his options in applying to medical schools. Recently, he visited some of the villages in Nigeria where his grandfather had established churches. Continuing that legacy is attractive to him.

"I don't want to presume about where the Lord will have me serve," he said. "I'll just wait and let God unfold it for me one piece at a time. I'm praying, 'God, just send me wherever I can be the most useful.'" His desire is to minister as a doctor to the people of Africa, where diseases such as AIDS are ravaging the population.

His heart is broken for those who live in the most difficult circumstances. "I don't want to live a life of ease while there are so many that are suffering," Samkon said. "I love America, but it's human nature in this culture that when things are going well for us personally, we forget that people have needs, and that life is so difficult in other parts of the world."

There is a picture that God has burned into Samkon's heart. He sees it when he closes his eyes at night, when the cheering crowd is quiet and the stadium's lights are dark. "I see an image of people living in absolute misery, with no hope and no future but to die and go to hell. God wants me to bring hope and healing to those people. He wants me to show them Jesus."

CHAPTER 6

May I Speak to the Person in Charge?

And how bold and free we then become in his presence, freely asking according to his will, sure that he's listening.
—1 John 5:14 (*The Message*)

It's not an oversimplification, but an absolute fact: There is no mission without prayer! God-given missions are born as a result of prayer, are directed by prayer, and are sustained by prayer. So God's priority for parents, as we seek to plant missional seeds in our children's lives, is to pray fervently for them.

That's not necessarily as easy as it sounds. Once we begin to get down to the real business of praying for our kids, we begin to discover that our efforts often seem completely inadequate. We pray that God would lead them, that He would bless them and that He would protect them. But, without those occasional bolts of godly insight to inspire us, our prayers often seem to settle into almost a repetitious "now-I-lay-me-down-to-sleep" routine. There must be more to it. These are children, God's most precious gifts, for whom we're praying. And we're praying about their decisions, their calling and their mission. So why do the words sometimes seem somewhat cold, almost scripted?

We would feel guilty about such an inequity, unless we realized that the shortcoming is not our lack of passion. The very fact that this is a concern of most parents bears that out. Instead, it may be our lack of knowledge of exactly what we should pray that causes that feeling of inadequacy.

In John 17, we get a glimpse of what Jesus considered a priority for his prayer life. In this most intimate moment with His Father, His prayer wasn't about His needs or what would make His life more comfortable. His prayer was entirely focused outward. It was all about others—His disciples. He understood His calling was to prepare His disciples for their mission. They were His spiritual offspring, so He offers us a unique perspective as to how we should pray for our own children and their mission in this world.

This important chapter reveals some distinct themes that Jesus believed to be vital to His disciples' calling. These are the same themes that make our prayers for our children alive and relevant. When we pray for our child's mission with this understanding within our spirit, it releases us to be sensitive to the particular areas of focus to which the Holy Spirit would want to lead us.

† Pray for their salvation (see John 17:2–3).

Our ultimate goal as parents is that our children experience a life-changing encounter with God through Jesus Christ. A poll by researcher George Barna revealed that nearly half (43 percent) of all Americans who accept Jesus Christ as their Savior do so before reaching the age of 13. That's an astounding finding, proving the importance of a child meeting Jesus at an early age.

The nature of that encounter in an adult's life often brings with it dramatic changes. But we shouldn't necessarily expect to see that kind of radical transformation when a child accepts Jesus. The process of salvation that happens within young hearts varies dramatically from child to child. Our tendency is to desire so greatly that our kids know Christ that we try to make it happen, and that's just not our job. Or we might expect a certain result when it does happen, not acknowledging that it's our child's experience, and it's unique from our own or anyone else's.

In His prayer, Jesus didn't try to define what others' experiences would look like. He didn't try to tell His Father how to make it happen. He simply prayed "that they may know you, the only true God, and Jesus Christ, whom you have sent." Day after day, the most glorious thing that we could hope to see in our children's lives is that they love Jesus more deeply, that they experience God more genuinely, and that the assurance of their salvation is more certain. What exactly, then, is our most important responsibility in that process? We must model for them a genuine vital relationship that we have with Christ—one that is so attractive that they want to experience it too.

† Pray for their growth and maturity (see John 17:4–10).

When our son Matt was in high school, he was an offensive lineman for one of the top football programs in the state of Texas. And if you know anything about Texas high school football, that really means something! He was coachable and he worked hard to make his techniques flawless. The problem was that Matt didn't have the size that an offensive lineman needs to have. And on a high school team where the rest of the offensive line averaged about 270 pounds, he was lagging far behind. He tried vitamin supplements blended in disgustingly chalky high-protein shakes, and he ate as much beef as he could devour in every sitting. But he still didn't gain weight. He was frustrated by the lack of success, and we felt badly for him. We would have done absolutely whatever it took, within the rules of high school football, to help him grow bigger.

> Hand-in-hand with our prayers is the care that we take to equip them.

If you had to observe a lack of spiritual growth in your offspring, it would be at least as discouraging. The ups and downs, the struggles to overcome and the lack of victories would be a source of anxiety for both the parents and the child.

Praying for our kids to mature in their relationship with Christ is essential. But hand-in-hand with our prayers is the care that we take to equip them for growth. Although they are valuable experiences, assuming that sending our children to Sunday School or enrolling them in Christian schools will expose them to knowledge of God and His Word is just not enough. It is one of our primary responsibilities to help our children daily fill their hearts and minds with God's Word and to help them understand how that applies to the moments and days that we live, even as Jesus did for His disciples.

Speaking of His followers, Jesus told His Father, "I gave them the words you gave me." He had diligently taught them all that God had intended for them. And then He prayed that those words would not be empty. Jesus' desire was that they had heard what He had spoken and applied those words in their lives toward spiritual growth and maturity.

The story of our relationship with God through Jesus Christ is meaningful. It demonstrates the reality and the faithfulness of our

Father. As we continue to grow along our journey, our children recognize just how relevant our thriving walk with God really is.

† Pray for their protection (see John 17:11b–12b)

Today's world can be a scary place to raise a child. But life has always been dangerous. In generations past, there were no cures for even the simplest diseases. Providing shelter from the elements at one time proved to be a challenge. As people of this nation moved westward, they lived with the threat of attacks from warlike tribes. The reality we must face is that we can never completely guard our children from danger, physically, psychologically, or spiritually.

Our daughter and son-in-law, Annie and Robbie, are walking through that right now. When our absolutely wonderful grandson, Josiah, was born, the doctors realized that he was having some digestion difficulties. He had serious surgery during the first week of his life. He recovered, but in the process was diagnosed with cystic fibrosis (CF). It was such a shock because he looked so healthy. For his mom and dad, and all the rest of us who love Josiah, fear kicked in. And with the fear, came the questions.

What happens to kids with CF? Is he going to make it?

Why would God allow this to happen to such a beautiful, innocent little baby?

We all received the wisdom and assurance of the doctors, and then we all seemingly simultaneously received godly inspiration—this was something that we all had to walk through day by day with Josiah. Trust God; He is big enough to take care of everything else. Thankfully, God is more than sufficient for any task. His Word assures us that we can prayerfully entrust our children into His hands.

God is our refuge and strength, an ever-present help in trouble. Therefore we will not fear, though the earth give way and the mountains fall into the heart of the sea, though its waters roar and foam and the mountains quake with their surging.
—Psalm 46:1–3 (NIV)

At each new step of their growing up, you're forced to trust God for your children's safety. One of the most difficult parenting experiences we encountered was when we drove away after leaving our kids at college. We had the most helpless feeling as we saw them in our rearview mirror standing there on that campus, waving good-bye. "What if?" became a thought that ran through our minds time after time. We could imagine all kinds of things that could go wrong as we were miles away from them. We had to face reality in order to maintain our sanity. We placed them again in God's hands, then purged our thoughts of all those negative imaginations. We just had to picture them every evening, right there in their dorm rooms, at the desk…studying. We still don't know how accurate that picture really was! But we do know that it allowed us to rest in the fact that God could take care of them much better than we could. So with our thought life under control and our imagination in check, we could pray confidently for God's protection over them.

† Pray for their mission (see John 17:15–18).

One of the primary components of Jesus' ministry was teaching His followers about their relationship to the rest of the world. He understood completely the dangers and the difficulties, and He prayed that His disciples would be protected from those things. But He also knew that their mission was in the world. They had been called to go into the world, into the teeth of whatever negative influences they would face, and show His love and His grace there.

The realization that our kids are called by God for His purposes is a big step in missional parenting. As we deal with all the usual uncertainties that accompany this process, praying for our child's mission provides not only the momentum for their ministry, but a source of encouragement and confidence for us, as parents.

As children begin to grow into their calling, there are certain special requirements for their mission:

- Wisdom can be defined as God's perspective. Wisdom protects our kids from being deceived and it gives them the tools to make right decisions.

- Self-discipline is the extension of parental correction. It's reasonable and consistent and results in a lifestyle of obedience to God and His direction.

- Confidence is the essence of commitment. When our children are confident in God and in their calling, they don't stagger in the face of difficulties.

Our prayer for our child's mission is not that we might have inspiration to draw up the blueprint for them. As Jesus prayed for His disciples, we ask God to produce wisdom, self-discipline, and confidence in them so that they are equipped for the task of discovering His will and following His ways.

† Pray for their influence (see John 17:18–21).

Jesus prayed not only for His disciples but for all those who would follow as a result of their ministry. He knew that God would lead His disciples to the places and the people who not only needed to be made whole, but to those who would respond to their own calling and mission.

Finding the delicate balance between responding to peoples' needs on our own, or at God's direction, is crucial to the effectiveness of all ministry. Praying for those that God places in our children's lives intensifies their influence. From their earliest expressions toward God, our kids need to be taught to turn their prayers outward, to pray as fervently for other people and their needs as we pray for our own. So it's reasonable that we should make it a priority to pray for the world where God has placed our children.

It's important that, as our children navigate their "missions field," that they learn to love the people they're led to. We pray that they become sensitive to others and that our children's hearts are tender toward those in need. And we pray that they would have clarity in knowing where God is leading them.

† Pray for wisdom in supporting them (see John 17:26).

Here's that "wisdom" thing again. But this time we're looking at it from a different perspective. What a blessing it is to have godly parents to offer encouragement and counsel! One of the toughest things for parents to do, though, is to know when and how to dispense all that wisdom that's inside our heads. Our love for our kids often produces an eagerness that causes us to speak and do before we think. And we all know the conflicts that can cause!

As our kids were growing up, that sharing of wisdom was the source of some irritation to them. Sometimes, we chose to give advice when we should have simply been a sounding board for what they were thinking. As they have become adults, Anne and Matt have learned to preface many of their discussions with us by saying, "I'm not asking you to do anything about this, I just want you to listen." It's difficult to make that gradual transformation, becoming what God wants us to be in our children's lives at each stage of their development.

Jesus asked His Father that His input would continue to be received by the disciples. His wisdom gave Him the right advice, the right questions, the right direction for each moment. He was led by God to sense and know not only what His disciples needed to know for their mission, but how to communicate it in a way that they would be open to it. Our prayer should be, as much as we desire to be sensitive to our kids, that we should be even more sensitive to God. His wisdom will lead us to be what our children need from us, exactly when they need it.

Prayer is our never-ending parental responsibility. There is not a moment during any day, through any stage of life from the time they are conceived, that our prayers are not the most significant investment that we make in our children. To make that responsibility relevant and alive assures that those prayers are meaningful and effective as they seek God's mission.

THINK

▲ Consider for a moment your prayers for your children. When compared to Jesus' prayer in John 17 for His disciples, is there a new focus or aspect that you might add to your prayers?

▲ Even though the WWJD craze might have become a bit trite with time, do I actually take opportunities to explore the question, *What would Jesus do?* with my family members, concerning situations in their lives?

DO TRY THIS AT HOME!

❏ Look through the different sections of Jesus' prayer for His disciples in John 17, and focus your prayer for your children and spouse on a different, specific aspect each day for a week. Make it a habit to consistently, consciously include these in your prayers for your family.

❏ As you ask family members to share details about their day, make it a practice to offer quick, simple prayers, asking aloud for God to give them wisdom to know His direction and willingness and courage to act accordingly in each situation.

LIVE IT!

"Frankly, these meetings are beginning to bore me," snorted Nachowr. "These are the most powerful men in the land, and King

Amon should do more to assure that everyone's happy. I've heard rumblings and complaining."

"So true. This wine is somewhat bitter, and I recognize some of these prostitutes from the last time we were here," Sharar added.

As was typical of these political gatherings of the king's advisers, the brief sessions of real business were followed by days of debauchery. Gluttonous feasting, heavy drinking and unbridled promiscuity were the actual focus. They chose to ignore the real problems that were facing the Kingdom of Judah. Within the nations surrounding their borders, radical changes were taking place. Uncertainty and instability were sweeping throughout the region. There were revolutions in progress, and the fragile peace and prosperity that the people of Judah had once enjoyed were quickly crumbling.

No one even noticed as one of King Amon's servants summoned Nachowr to the corner of the room. His face was ashen when he returned to his seat and delivered the shocking news: "King Amon has been assassinated!"

Nachowr suddenly felt faint. His head was spinning as he began to digest the news. "What happens now?" he thought. Josiah, Amon's son, was only eight years old. But, he was to be the new King of Judah. All Nachowr could think of was how this might affect his own foothold in the power structure of the palace. Could an eight-year-old actually rule?

After a few years had passed and the initial shock of the assassination had faded, Nachowr and many of the others in the council decided that having a boy king wasn't such a bad idea. "Of course, he's just a figurehead," Nachowr reasoned with Sharar. "We have the real power."

But the power the government held was unsettled. The conditions of the nation had become deplorable. Anarchy filled the land of Judah. It was "every man for himself," as greed, jealousy, and depravity had overtaken everyone's sensibilities.

Sharar shrugged. "I'm just not certain I want this responsibility on my shoulders any longer. Judah could be in real trouble. Our economy is suffering, and the people are restless. King Josiah is asking too many questions. And he's spending too much time with those religious fools. He's actually started to listen to them."

Nachowr had noticed that, too. "He's a teenager now. Maybe if we included him in some of our 'meetings'..."

"I don't think so," said Sharar. "He thinks that may be our problem. That's what the prophets are telling him."

Josiah had always been a curious boy. Since he was small, he had asked so many questions. Those who were assigned the task of caring for him usually lost their patience and tried to occupy his time with trivial matters—mindless games and jokes that seemed to satisfy most kids. But not Josiah.

When he became king, he listened, even though he was a child. He heard discussions about the conditions of the nations surrounding Judah, and the economic difficulty that could overtake the Hebrews because of it. He sensed fear throughout the kingdom. Josiah began to seek information and advice from the elder statesmen. He wanted to know more about Hebrew history, government, and religion. He also wanted to know all he could about his great-grandfather Hezekiah and his ancestors, especially King David. Some older people vaguely recalled legendary accounts of David's life—stories about a giant, wild animals, and lots of music. Josiah was intrigued by what he heard, especially the stories of his ancestors' unshakable belief in Jehovah.

Josiah had become especially close to the high priest, Hilkiah, and his son, Jeremiah. They were godly people, and Josiah trusted their judgment.

"Hilkiah, what would cause men like David and Hezekiah to dedicate themselves completely to a deity that they couldn't even see?" Josiah asked the high priest.

"Once they experienced a relationship with the one true God, they felt compelled to be committed to Him," explained Hilkiah. "They desired above all else to serve and obey His law."

Jeremiah agreed. "That's what our nation needs, Josiah. We need to rediscover what our ancestors experienced. There was a holy temple here where they worshipped Jehovah. And it was a sacred place, nothing like the shameful temples we have today."

"What if," Josiah reasoned, "our salvation as a nation lies somewhere in that rubble of those times past?"

With a redirected focus, Josiah called in engineers and historians, questioning them about the places that once were significant for the Hebrews but were now broken down ruins.

"We will begin by cleansing Judah of all the idols," Josiah proclaimed. "Then we will rebuild the Temple where our forefathers worshipped Jehovah."

The task of ridding the land of the depravity that had swallowed it up was a huge undertaking for anyone, much less a teenager. But Josiah wasn't like the other Hebrew teens. Instead of all the frivolous things that most of them dabbled in, he had immersed himself in being a king and crying out to Jehovah to bring peace and blessing back to his people.

Josiah persevered in the face of a hurting, doubting population. He was determined to share with all the people of Judah that Jehovah was the one true God. Boldly, he invited the citizens to hear about what he had learned. Josiah urged them to repent and seek God, just as he had. They heard the passion in his voice, sensed his deep conviction and were stirred. "Could the king be right about this Jehovah?" they asked. They wanted it to be true, but how could they be certain?

As Josiah poured out his heart to a large group of the Hebrew people one day, he spotted the scribe Shaphan, one of his closest confidants, eagerly pressing through the crowd. He was waving a scroll above his head and calling out to Josiah. Although he couldn't hear exactly what Shaphan was saying, Josiah knew that it must be something important because Shaphan's eyes were open wide.

"Josiah! We found it!" shouted Shaphan. "This is it! We found it where we're rebuilding the temple!"

"Shaphan, come here! Tell me what's going on!"

"These scrolls! King Josiah, this is the Law of Moses! It's all right here, exactly what we thought all along. Jehovah had a plan for our people, and we are so far away from it. But now, we know that this is the truth and that He is real, the Almighty God!"

As Josiah read Jehovah's law aloud, he wept and cried out to God for forgiveness. "Jehovah God, have mercy on me and the people of Judah!"

He began to tear his royal robes, overwhelmed by the power of God's Word. The people were shaken by the enormity of this moment with their king, and they began to fervently seek God also.

It was the beginning of the restoration of the nation of Judah. Though their sins and neglect of the past would bring them grief, they had found their way back into the arms of Jehovah. God had chosen a small boy to become king for this moment. He had sensed the tenderness of Josiah's heart and the genuineness of his character. He didn't need power or stature to break through to His people. He found all He needed in a little child.

(Based on 2 Kings 22–23)

CHAPTER 7

Louder Than Words

If I could speak all the languages of earth and of angels, but didn't love others, I would only be a noisy gong or a clanging cymbal.
—1 Corinthians 13:1 (NLT)

You know the story of what happened in Judea. It began in Galilee after John preached a total life-change. Then Jesus arrived from Nazareth, anointed by God with the Holy Spirit, ready for action. He went through the country helping people and healing everyone who was beaten down by the Devil. He was able to do all this because God was with him.
—Acts 10:37–38 (*The Message*)

When your mother admonished you with the old adage "Actions speak louder than words," she was actually laying out an important scriptural principle. We don't seem to focus on it enough, but Jesus' identity in His world was as a selfless servant. He didn't travel from place to place with some superstar status. The disciples weren't an entourage. He didn't simply feel compassion for people, shake his head, click his tongue, and move to the next place.

Jesus was a doer. His purpose in life was to help others—everyone, everywhere, no matter what the cost. He knew that pouring His life into others was the cornerstone of everything that He wanted to share with them. With the ultimate example being Jesus' way of life and His death on the Cross, we need to help our family learn that the world often won't give us the privilege of sharing the Word until we've won that right with our service.

Serving others in Jesus' world loses something in translating it into today's culture. We can try to justify our hesitancy to reach out with a multitude of excuses. In the twenty-first century, our self-sufficiency and isolation build walls. Skepticism won't always allow full access. And, besides, aren't people really supposed to be taken care of by professionals in government programs and nonprofit organizations?

But the fact is, serving others is commanded. It's our calling. God expects it. And, Jesus lived it. There are real families today living it also. We talked to many of our friends around the world who have a Jesus heart for serving others. They've engaged their entire family in bringing Christ's love to their communities by serving others, and it's working, for them and for their world. Probably the best way to learn what serving others can look like for your family is to see just what it looks like in these homes. So, via email, they shared with us their creativity and their commitment, and we hope it sparks something within you, too. Though the culture has changed remarkably since then, Jesus' life provided eternal principles about how we should serve. These families caught on to what He did, and they are taking it to heart.

Jesus was INTENTIONAL

> *Your attitude should be the same as that of Christ Jesus: Who, being in very nature God, did not consider equality with God something to be grasped, but made himself nothing, taking the very nature of a servant, being made in human likeness.*
> —Philippians 2:5–7 (NIV)

Serving others is a choice that we make. As a family, we must intentionally decide that serving will define who we are. That decision is established by making the commitment to do and to serve and, then, diligently following through with it. But it's reinforced by stating and discussing again and again that serving is your identity as a family. "We serve others," is a verbal determination that secures your family's spiritual DNA. And when that happens, the selfless attitude that Jesus demonstrated creates who you really become.

This email tells how servant hearts became a generational legacy:

From: deborah m
To: martha and greg
Subject: Soup
Andrea and I make chicken soup for a sick friend or if there has been a death in the family. We shop together and prepare and deliver it together. Zach will come with us to deliver the meal. My mother did this, and I wanted to pass it along to my kids. My mom used to make everything homemade—the soup, the bread, the dessert, everything. Well, I still make the soup, but I buy the dessert and bread, and I don't feel guilty in the least!

When your family is intentional about serving, even seemingly insignificant events trigger thoughts about doing for others.

From: Ted
To: Martha and Greg
Subject: The sweater
This family tradition was actually started in a large Sunday School class I taught (a singles class with over 2,000 members, but average attendance of about 700...fun class), but it has become an occasional standard for my family.

I found a hole in my favorite sweater one icy Sunday morning while I was getting ready for church and the class I was to teach. I threw it away almost immediately, but then felt that I should take it with me to class. I thought there might be a message in finding a hole in my seven-year-old favorite sweater.

I took it to the class, talked about the inconveniences and frustrations that enter our lives and told the class that I intended to give it to a homeless person when I left the church. Then I suggested, "Why don't you go home and find the coats that have shrunk due to darkness in your closet, meet me at Denny's for coffee and pie, and we can take the coats to the Presbyterian Night Shelter." That afternoon, we delivered more than 75 coats to the shelter, enjoyed coffee and pecan pie together and went home to our fireplaces and football games.

Now that my sons are grown and live nearby, we often call them on cold days, invite them over for coffee and pie, suggest that they find the shrunken coats...theirs and the grandchildren's, and we deliver them to the shelter.

Jesus was AVAILABLE

Sitting down, Jesus called the Twelve and said, "If anyone wants to be first, he must be the very last, and the servant of all." He took a little child and had him stand among them. Taking him in his arms, he said to them, "Whoever welcomes one of these little children in my name welcomes me; and whoever welcomes me does not welcome me but the one who sent me."
—Mark 9:35–37 (NIV)

Jesus was always ready for action. What a dynamic way to live your life! He was constantly aware that He was called to serve, because He had already determined that that was who He was. He knew well that a life of service calls us to be revolutionary in the way we approach day-to-day living. When our thoughts about being a servant are geared in that direction, we don't waste time and effort deciding whether or not we should respond to a particular need. A servant's heart is rarely overwhelmed by the enormity of the need. Servants aren't paralyzed by those situations; they are doers, like Jesus.

Franklin Graham is the director of Samaritan's Purse, an organization that serves in very practical ways those in need, in desperate circumstances and in the midst of tragedy and disaster. Even Graham was stunned, though, when he observed firsthand the devastation of Hurricane Katrina on the Gulf Coast in 2005.

"When we first arrived and saw the overwhelming destruction, many people asked where you even begin to respond," said Graham. "It starts with helping just one person, one family at a time, and doing what we can to give people relief and a sense of hope."

Your family can start there, too—helping one person or one other family. Then begin to create that identity, that you are doers, servers, a family that gives hope to those who need it most.

The Thanksgiving and Christmas seasons provide a great opportunity for you to serve others.

From: Kenn
To: Martha & Greg
Subject: Thanksgiving bags
As a whole family, we were part of a mass-assembly of

Thanksgiving dinner bags. We worked with several other families to make sure that each bag had a frozen turkey and all the necessary fixin's. Then, as a family, we would go out and present these dinners in a bag to families identified through our church as being in need. We did this at Christmas, too, and we took gifts along with the food.

Have you ever hesitated giving to someone in need because you fear they might not use what you give them responsibly? This email offers a solution!

From: Lori
To: Martha and Greg
Subject: Serving others
We try to keep a few brown lunch bags w/ some foods & small water bottle in it. Things that last awhile & don't "spoil" in the car…and whenever we come to a stoplight that has someone standing there "collecting" from the cars, the kids get really excited to give out one of our bags…it helps us help people without worrying about how they might spend cash if we give it to them…and provides for their immediate need for food & water.

Jesus was INVISIBLE
He won't call attention to what he does with loud speeches or gaudy parades. He won't brush aside the bruised and the hurt and he won't disregard the small and insignificant, but he'll steadily and firmly set things right.
—Isaiah 42:2–4 (*The Message*)

The prophet Isaiah captured the very essence of who Jesus was centuries before He actually began serving others. Jesus didn't want recognition. He didn't even desire to teach a lesson. He simply wanted to bring love to the unlovable and dignity to those crushed by the weight of the world.

Christian sociologist and professor Tony Campolo has, for a number of years, been a voice that challenged the church to become true servants. And he takes it a step further in challenging us to do it without fanfare.

"Another way of helping the poor is to give them what they need, but never let them know where it came from," Campolo said.

"That's why I get very upset with youth groups that deliver food baskets and toys at Christmas to poor families and stand around and sing Christmas carols. Please, I want them to deliver the toys and the food. I just don't want them to hang around. Leave the stuff on the back steps, run away, call the people on the phone and tell them, 'There is stuff on the back steps. It's for you! This is God.' And hang up."

As Scott relates next, your children will remember your selfless acts of service.

From: Scott in North Carolina
To: Martha & Greg
Subject: Serving
Some of the most poignant memories of serving those "in need" was helping people we knew do things that they couldn't do for themselves. Dad had a pickup truck, and more than once we went and helped people move furniture. We would do odd jobs around people's houses (painting, repairing fences, mowing lawns, cleaning gutters, etc.), and usually, Mom would bake some bread (not some coordinated effort when a bunch of other people were there) and make a casserole or something for them. This impressed me, as a child, as an "invisible" act of compassion and love like Jesus would have done. There wasn't any room for the mutual "attaboys." In fact there was an unspoken understanding where we wouldn't tell anybody that they couldn't do these things for themselves and they wouldn't tell anyone we helped."

Jesus was PRACTICAL

"Then the King will say to those on his right, 'Come, you who are blessed by my Father; take your inheritance, the kingdom prepared for you since the creation of the world. For I was hungry and you gave me something to eat, I was thirsty and you gave me something to drink, I was a stranger and you invited me in, I needed clothes and you clothed me, I was sick and you looked after me, I was in prison and you came to visit me.'

"Then the righteous will answer him, 'Lord, when did we see you hungry and feed you, or thirsty and give you something to drink? When did we see you a stranger and invite you in, or needing clothes and clothe you? When did we see you sick or in prison and go to visit you?'

"The King will reply, 'I tell you the truth, whatever you did for one of the least of these brothers of mine, you did for me.'"
—Matthew 25:34–40 (NIV)

You and your family don't have to wait for the "big things" to come along in order to be servants. In fact, it's the most obvious needs that are addressed on a consistent basis that create a Christlike attitude in your and your children's hearts.

Jesus pointed out that even the most astute don't always understand the dynamics of servanthood. He said that providing for the practical needs of others is as if we are actually serving Him.

> Even the most astute don't always understand the dynamics of servanthood.

We receive our inheritance as God's children, Jesus said, when we participate in God's kingdom by giving of ourselves to others.

There is no lack of people in need in our world today. And though many of the needs seem overwhelming, Jesus implores us not to overlook the simple things—food for the hungry, a drink for the thirsty, clothing for the impoverished, and attending to those who can't help themselves.

We received so many responses from families who were, in the course of their everyday living, meeting practical needs of others.

> From: pat w
> To: marthaandgreg
> Subject: gloves
> We have been gathering up gloves and hats for children in need at an elementary school. Over the last several years, we have been able to give around 300 pairs of gloves and hats to help those precious little ones keep their hands and heads warm.

Most of us understand there's a need to assist those that are obviously poor in our communities. But sometimes, we overlook the needs of others that may be closer to home.

> From: Dede
> To: Martha and Greg
> Subject: Mom and Dad

I remember Mom and Dad would "take pity," I guess you could say, on the seminary students who came to our church. I remember Lou and Mary, and a fellow from China whose name I think was Onu, or something like that, and a host of others. Realizing that most of them were living very frugally, Mom and Dad would ask them over for Sunday lunch. It was good for them to have a nice meal and a family atmosphere, but it was also good for me and my sister to sit at the feet of people from whom we could gain insight and wisdom.

There are ways to include the entire family in our serving and giving. Through them, our kids' lives may be impacted forever.

From: Wanda
To: Martha and Greg
Subject: Serving others
 We put together bags of hygiene products to give to local homeless shelters. The packets contained full-size shampoo, bar of soap and soap dish, brush, comb, toothpaste, toothbrush, lotion and deodorant. The idea was that each "guest" at a shelter could receive his or her own packet of products to clean up with. Each packet also contained a Bible and a package of underwear. We had the kids buy the underwear in their own size. It impacted the children to put "child-size" underwear into their packets and have an understanding that there were children their age and size that didn't have a home or bed.

Jesus was SACRIFICIAL
Just as the Son of Man did not come to be served, but to serve and to give his life as a ransom for many.
—Matthew 20:28 (NIV)

Is serving really serving unless it costs us something? Jesus gave up everything, His life, to serve us. So what is He asking you and your family to sacrifice in order to serve others? Is it your spare time that you sometimes guard too selfishly? Is He asking that you give from your pocket more liberally? Could there be something else in your life that holds you back from serving others?

The principle is unmistakable and undeniable. To be like Christ, we have to be willing to put aside all pride and all comfort to serve others.

To: The Singletons
Subject: Helping the Homeless
My family would go to the homeless shelter and serve the meals to the people there. We kids were uncomfortable at first—it wasn't "cool" and we thought somebody might see us there. But as time went on, we began to really look forward to going to help.

We are all aware of the importance of "family time," when we gather together just to be with each other. It's a good and necessary thing, but what if sometimes God asked us to even sacrifice some of those times to include others like students or military personnel who are away from their own homes?

From: The Cassettas
To: Martha & Greg
Subject: Students for the holidays
We have international college students over for Thanksgiving, and it is a great experience. They really appreciate being part of a family for holidays. They're very curious about American home life and customs but often don't have an opportunity to see the inside of an American home. It is also a great chance to expose our kids to another culture. Kids tend to build bridges quickly and make the whole experience much easier and more enjoyable for all. So that's one idea for ministering as a family that has worked for us.

The adventure of serving others promises to make an eternal impact on you and your children. It serves as an example of what being like Jesus really looks like. When it's something that your family has never done before, it can be intimidating, but the reward is rich and well worth the step of faith that it requires. Immerse your family in prayer, leading them to ask God how He's calling you to serve. Then trust that He will provide the opportunities, the courage, and the confidence to touch your world!

 THINK

▲ What are some specific needs that I'm aware of in our neighborhood? Our church? Our city? Around the world?

▲ What are two actions we could perform for another person or family, with no strings attached, that would serve them or help them in some way? What's keeping us from doing these things?

━━ ━━ **DO** TRY THIS AT HOME! ━━ ━━

A Vision for the World
❏ Did you know that a goat costs only $75? In the World Vision gift catalog, you can buy one for a family in places like Haiti or Kenya and it will provide much needed food, an income, and fertilizer for their crops. World Vision is respected around the world for their dedicated missions work worldwide and for their financial accountability. Their Web site, www.worldvision.org, is particularly user-friendly and offers some great opportunities for giving for your family. Not only can you find a child to sponsor according to their location, age and other specifics, you can also browse through their gift catalog in order to donate. With specific gifts, like goats, chickens and school supplies that can be given to others around the world, your whole family can be actively engaged in giving to those in need. The products illustrate the needs and you're able to understand exactly how you can help. At the World Vision Web site, explore the "Ways to Give" section for some great service ideas in which your entire family can participate.

On Your Heart
❏ Ask each family member what they think is the greatest need around the world. Encourage them to go into detail by asking:
  ◆ "How do you feel about that?"
  ◆ "What makes you feel so strongly about it?"
  ◆ "What needs to happen in that situation?"
  ◆ "What can we do to help?"

❏ Serve somewhere together!
  ◆ Discuss together what your family can do to serve others right in your community. Encourage everyone to participate in the discussion and allow everyone's ideas to be considered. It makes it more exciting if you write the ideas on butcher paper or poster board as you're talking, then hang them on the walls so your family can just soak it in for a few days.

❏ Some more great opportunities
  ◆ Angel Tree
  ◆ www.angeltree.org
  ◆ Angel Tree reaches out to the children of prisoners and their families with the love of Christ. During Christmas, they deliver gifts in the name of their parents.

❏ Samaritan's Purse
  ◆ www.samaritanspurse.org
  ◆ Samaritan's Purse aids the world's poor, sick, and suffering. They are an effective means of reaching hurting people in countries around the world with food, medicine, and other assistance in the name of Jesus Christ.

❏ Operation Blessing
  ◆ www.ob.org
  ◆ Since 1978, Operation Blessing International has touched the lives of more than 209.3 million people in 105 countries and all 50 states, providing goods and services valued at more than $1.7 billion.

❏ Ask your pastor about other local and worldwide organizations that your church recommends for your gifts and service.

▦ ▦ ▦ LIVE IT! ▦ ▦ ▦

Like most younger brothers, he knew all the buttons to push. He was brash and bold, even to the point of being overconfident. He was forever spinning all those wild tales of his adventures while he was tending the sheep. And almost every day, he wanted all his brothers to listen to the new music that he had just composed. But, as irritating as David could be at times, Eliab still loved him and felt responsible for looking out for him. That's why, when David showed up on the battlefield that day, Eliab couldn't believe his eyes. He spotted his little brother, in the middle of all the soldiers, bothering them with all his questions and then giving them his unsolicited opinions about how he would handle things if he were a soldier.

"David! What are you doing here?"

"Dad sent me to find out how you're doing. And he wanted me to bring you this." He handed Eliab a basket of bread and cheese from home.

"I know you, David. You just came here to be close to all the excitement," Eliab said.

"What do you suppose King Saul would do for the man who killed that giant, Goliath?" asked David with that familiar glint in his eye.

"Don't even think about it!" Eliab said. "You're still just a kid. You have no idea about how dangerous Goliath is. Go back home before you get into trouble."

"Eliab, isn't there a cause to fight for? Listen to all the trash he's talking about our people and our God," David said. "We can't just sit back and take that. You're all hiding while he threatens everything we believe in and everything we've lived for. If nobody else is man enough to do it, then I'll challenge him!"

When the other soldiers heard David's confident claims, they were more than happy to escort him to King Saul, relieving themselves of the certainty of defeat and death in confronting Goliath. Eliab pressed through the crowd of soldiers to get a glimpse of his little brother in the presence of royalty.

The whole scene would have been almost comical if the situation hadn't been so grave. There was David, swallowed up in Saul's armor, standing before the king, pleading his case. The big bronze helmet rested on David's shoulders, and the breastplate forced his arms almost straight out from his body.

"I cannot let you go out there and battle that giant," said King Saul. "Look at you! You're just a boy!"

David peered from under the brim of the helmet, looked Saul squarely in the eyes and said, "I know I'm young. But while I've tended my father's sheep, I've killed lions and bears that have tried to attack the flock. I just grabbed them by the hair and slugged them and they fell over dead."

"Oh no!" thought Eliab. "It's those wild animal stories again. And listen to his voice! He's not even through puberty and the more excited he gets, the more it's cracking! How embarrassing!"

David took another step closer to the king. "King Saul," he said soberly, "I don't do these things alone. God has delivered me from each one of these dangers. And, now, I go before the giant, Goliath, not on my own, but in the name of the Living God, and He will deliver me and our people from the hand of this Philistine."

Saul had not seen such sincere confidence in trained warriors twice David's age. He spoke with such authority that the king himself was moved. The boy had not only restored Saul's own determination, he had also renewed his faith. Despite the fact that

David was a mere boy, how could he deny him the opportunity to fulfill his calling?

Saul sighed, shook his head and said, "Go ahead, David, and may God be with you."

"One more thing," said David. "Would you get all this armor off me? I can't even move."

Eliab watched his youngest brother stride down the hillside toward Goliath, the giant Philistine. He swallowed hard, fearful of what could happen. After all, David was confronting this huge man, an enemy, who was fully armed and experienced in warfare. And he was only a boy with a slingshot and a few rocks.

As David drew closer to the giant, Goliath saw that the Hebrews had chosen to confront him with this boy. He began to chide him and his people. His booming voice spewed curses on David and the Hebrew's God. Goliath's menacing laugh echoed across the battlefield, "Come here, boy. Let me feed your flesh to the birds."

David bristled and his steely eyes glared at Goliath. "You come at me with all your weapons of warfare," he said, "but I come at you in the name of the Lord Almighty. He will deliver you into my hands today, and the whole world is going to know that there is a God in Israel."

"Amazing!" said Eliab under his breath. He had never seen anyone, much less his own flesh and blood, exude such confidence! Suddenly, he no longer feared for David's life. Instead, he believed in David's cause. If David were able to risk life and limb for what he believed in, then he was inspired to do the same.

"Everyone watch this and know one thing for sure," David said to all those gathered around. "God doesn't need a sword to win the battle, because the victory already belongs to Him."

Goliath decided he'd had enough of this smart-mouthed kid's disrespect. With a roaring battle cry, fueled by his anger, he lurched across the battlefield toward David. David took a rock, loaded his slingshot, and in one fluid motion flung it toward the charging giant. A dull thud silenced Goliath's shout. He stopped and fell at David's feet, the ground almost shaking from the collapse of his huge, lifeless body.

The entire battleground grew quiet as both armies tried to fathom what they had just witnessed. The mighty Goliath was dead, brought down by a boy with a slingshot and an unwavering confidence in God. The Philistines backed away slowly at first, but with the full realization that their intimidating leader was dead, they turned and ran home as fast as their feet could take them. The army of Israel went in hot pursuit and began to overtake them and slay them.

Eliab's head was spinning from what had taken place. He ran toward David and threw his arms around him, partly in celebration and partly in relief. As he embraced his brother, he saw him as he never had before. It was almost like he was a completely different person. He wasn't just his little brother any longer. He was courageous and bold. His own faith in God had been stirred by David's words, filled with authority and confidence. David was a man with a cause!

(Based on 1 Samuel 17)

The Fear Factor

"If you try to hang on to your life, you will lose it. But if you give up your life for my sake, you will save it."
—Matthew 16:25 (NLT)

"They who can give up essential liberty to obtain a little temporary safety, deserve neither liberty nor safety."
—Benjamin Franklin

If you're suffering from a low level of patriotism, let us prescribe a generous dose of Philadelphia.

Be sure you're equipped with some good walking shoes as you make your way through the downtown streets there, because once you begin your tour, it's difficult to finally declare that you've had enough. You make your way into buildings that bring those history textbooks to life—Independence Hall, where our nation was born; Carpenter's Hall where the First Continental Congress met in secret; Christ Church, which counted the Benjamin Franklin family and George and Martha Washington among its members; Betsy Ross's home; and the City Tavern, where the founding fathers met to discuss the day's current events. Not one of these buildings, in itself, is really very impressive by its design or decor. They are simple, relatively small buildings, made up of small rooms. But big ideas found their roots there.

Consider the commitments that were made in those places. The signers of the Declaration of Independence promised: "For the support of this Declaration, with a firm reliance on the protection of Divine Providence, we mutually pledge to each other our lives, our fortunes, and our sacred honor." And that was the price most of them had to pay in order to secure the liberty that we enjoy today.

What level of courage are we nurturing in the lives of our children today? Is it deep enough that they take a stand if they are challenged? If nobody else is willing to resist in the face of oppression, will they be bold enough to speak up? Will they be firm in protecting their faith and freedom? What if fear overcomes the boldness that it takes to go wherever God calls them?

Other than general apathy, perhaps the biggest deterrent to living a missional lifestyle is fear. There are, certainly, many dangerous perils in our culture if we focus on the "giants in the land." As parents, our tendency is to shield our family from difficult things. Suffering, of any kind, hurts. And it really hurts to see our own flesh and blood go through difficult things. So, we reason, the way to avoid it is to avoid the challenges.

The problem, though, is that God never promised that we would enjoy a stress-free easy life once we became a Christian. In several places in the Scripture, however, we are promised that the more closely we follow Christ, the more we will assuredly share in His suffering. But as much as we feel we should shield our loved ones from all the tough stuff, adversity and suffering aren't necessarily bad things. God has a distinct plan for each being that He has created. Fulfillment is found there. And, despite difficult circumstances and hurtful situations, there's a deep satisfaction as we walk in that calling. So, if we really want the very best for our children, we instinctively know that there may be tough things for them to face and difficult decisions that they have to make.

The missional Christian realizes that life lived Christ's way is an adventure, not for the timid. Jesus told us that we should be willing to "take up our cross" as we follow Him. The story of Paul includes shipwrecks, an escape in a basket, and imprisonment. The roster of the heroes of the faith includes many throughout history who gave their lives for what they believed.

Of course, we have an obligation to protect our children from danger, but not from experiences that may help them discover God's mission for their lives. And, certainly, we don't want to create within them a spirit of fear that paralyzes them, keeping them from achieving everything God gifted them to do. Christ's perfect love casts out fear, and our purpose as parents is to give our children the confidence in God to fearlessly follow where He leads. That can only be done if we parent courageously.

However, when it comes to finding that balance, the lines become a bit blurry. There's no perfect formula for how parents can keep their children safe and at the same time allow them to face challenges and grow in godly courage. It comes down to each individual situation that each individual child faces. And that calls for some hard work, tireless attention, and dedicated discipline by parents.

Thankfully, we do have some help in navigating this important aspect of creating courageous kids. Scripture offers some principles that reveal God's heart concerning this. And it's all about trusting Him.

Read the story of Abraham and his son, Isaac, in Genesis 22:1–18. God miraculously blessed Abraham and Sarah with a son, the fulfillment of a promise. Then, when Isaac was a young man, God told Abraham to take him and sacrifice him.

It's a familiar story that presents some interesting questions. Theologically, all those provocative discussions continue about why this story happened just this way. The principles of trust, though, revealed in the relationships between God, Abraham, and Isaac are much simpler. They provide a guideline about how parents can courageously navigate their family's way through difficult things rather than going around them and missing the center of God's purposes.

Trusting God's promise

One of the foundations of courageous parenting is a clear understanding concerning the promises that God makes about your children. In Genesis 17, when God first told Abraham that he and Sarah were going to have a son, Abraham laughed. It was a natural reaction, since he was 99 years old at the time. But God reassured him that there was a purpose for this child, and that through Isaac an entire nation would be established.

Imagine how Abraham felt then, when God told Him that he was to offer Isaac as a sacrifice. Would the promise die right there on the altar? Abraham had to be so certain of God's promise to him and to Isaac that, somehow, He knew what was going on. Greater than any situation that he faced, Abraham trusted that when God made a promise, He would be faithful to stand by it.

Your children are no less called by God than Isaac was. They are the fulfillment of God's promise to you that the faith that lives in you is worth passing on to another generation. When we declare how precious our new baby is, we're usually referring to the sweetness and innocence that we see in that little life. God calls them precious because that life is the culmination of an eternal design and an infinite love, brought into the world for His purpose. As much as we love our children and desire the very best for them, God's passion far exceeds ours.

Trusting God's protection

What do you suppose went through Abraham's mind as he made his way to the mountain with Isaac? Scripture doesn't record any questions or hesitation on Abraham's behalf, but our human nature would have certainly caused us to wonder whether we were actually hearing from God. Even if Abraham had been confused by God's direction, he somehow came to the conclusion that the right thing to do was trust his Heavenly Father. God had proven His faithfulness to protect Abraham and his family over and over again, so Abraham chose not to fear.

Let's be very honest with ourselves. Realistically measuring the risks involved in any situation is difficult, especially when it concerns our family. We have to acknowledge that life hurts sometimes. And in order to accomplish what we know needs to be done, risks are often involved. Our responsibility as parents in this matter is that we must be diligent and attentive to our family and also to ourselves. We must weigh challenges that our children might face and determine how—or even if—we should confront them on their behalf. There are the obvious ones from which we must protect our family at all costs. But there are also those difficult circumstances that bring maturity and growth in our children. We need to carefully evaluate those situations as to what the extent of our intervention should be.

Our thoughts get us in the most trouble when it comes to this aspect of trusting God. We seem to be able to build the most formidable scenarios of danger, one "what if" laid upon the next. Most of us parents do an excellent job of it.

We're thankful for cell phones. Had it not been for the fact that we provided them for our kids and they used them readily, there was no telling what kinds of trouble we would have concocted for them in our heads when they were away from us. We had a rule for our teenagers: if there was ever a change of plans when they were out, they must call and let us know the details. When we knew just where they were, who they were with, and what time they would be home, we were spared all the gruesome plots of our unchecked imagination.

Fear becomes the dominant force in our parenting style when we allow our thought life to control us. Fear trumps trust every time. If the cloud of fear covers our home, our family becomes isolated and one-dimensional. We can imagine all kinds of things that could happen to our kids. If our dark imagination, then, becomes the rudder that controls our parenting style, it can easily become a stumbling block as our children seek God's mission for their lives. There is no disease more contagious than fear, and your family will feel it and respond to it. Too often, a home controlled by fear produces kids who either cower and refuse to face challenges, or rebel and take on unnecessary risks.

> Trusting Him, we are free to parent courageously.

Thankfully, God has an answer. He tells us to bring our thought life under the control of the Holy Spirit, focus on Him, and trust His ability to care for our family.

> *Fix your thoughts on what is true, and honorable, and right, and pure, and lovely, and admirable. Think about things that are excellent and worthy of praise. Keep putting into practice all you learned and received from me—everything you heard from me and saw me doing. Then the God of peace will be with you.*
> —Philippians 4:8–9 (NLT)

Trusting Him, we are free to parent courageously. We serve as an example to our family that inspires them to reach beyond the easy things in order to conquer challenges. That kind of heart says yes when God speaks.

Trusting God's provision
When God proved Himself to Abraham, he was moved to name that very spot for what he had experienced there. Scripture tells us he called it "God will provide." That really wasn't a new revelation to Abraham. As he and Isaac made their way to the mountain, Isaac

asked him where the sacrifice was. Abraham, though he couldn't see the end from there, was certain of God's faithfulness and assured Isaac that God would provide the sacrifice.

There are many times during our lives that our family seems to be on a journey toward that mountain. We're not certain as to what will happen ahead of us. Financially, despite our plans for our children's future, there will be times the future is unclear. Our trust must be completely in God and His provision for us. There may be opportunities that become available that would enhance our family's calling—missions trips, special seminars, or family projects—and schedules and daily obligations seem to put them out of reach. But, like Abraham, when we focus on God's faithfulness, we can trust that He will provide. His provision might not always be exactly what we had mapped out, but we can know that He will always come through with what we need.

God's purposes for your children are amazing. He will protect the planning and abilities that He has invested in their lives. Our job is to trust that He will not leave the job undone when we are intentional about being obedient to follow where He leads our family.

The greatest tragedy will be if there is ever a generation that is paralyzed by fear. If comfort and security ever become more important than the call to become what we were created to be, the priority of God's mission for our lives, both faith and freedom will crumble.

There is something more important than possessions, status, or even happiness. That is the realization that life and liberty themselves are of the greatest value. We must teach our children that preserving those things that others have paid for is worth everything. The freedom that our founding fathers sacrificed to give us our freedom is most certainly a treasure. But the salvation that Christ gave us through His own blood, and the investment He has made in each life in order to fulfill His mission, is worth even more. It's worth everything.

 THINK

▲ In my own relationship with the Lord, what was the result of the challenges and trials I have faced? Did they make my faith stronger, or weaker? Where might I be today, if not for those challenges?

▲ Can I trust God to lead and guide my child as faithfully as He has done for me?

▲ What might I need to change about my approach that would allow God to strengthen my child's faith and personal experience with Him?

DO TRY THIS AT HOME!

What time I am afraid, I will put my trust in Thee.
—Psalm 56:3 (KJV)

❏ As a family, make this a memory verse. Then, over a period of days or weeks, let each person talk about "what times" they have been afraid. How did God take care of you in those situations? Guide the conversation from "things that go bump in the night," which is where most children may want to begin, to topics like fear of failure, lack of confidence, and giving in to peer pressure.

GOOGLE THIS:

What does the Bible say about fear?

LIVE IT!

Though he is not tall, he has the build and the gracefulness of the former college football and track star that he is. Some would say that he walks with a little swagger.

His eyes twinkle. He laughs easily and often.

And when he talks to people about Jesus, he does so with confidence and a natural authority.

Jeff is a youth pastor, and today he is on the otherwise deserted track, working with a high school athlete who has asked for Jeff's help in increasing his speed in the 40-yard dash for football.

"Let's just start by letting me see you run," Jeff says. "You take off, and I'll run along beside you."

"OK," Steve agrees, and the two take off around the track.

Running neck and neck, Jeff suddenly leans in, and Steve goes tumbling.

"Hey, what did you do that for?" Steve asks as he picks himself up off the ground, grinning sheepishly.

"You are running out of balance," Jeff tells him. "You've got to work on your arm placement and your leg movement, and keep everything in rhythm. Let's go again, and this time watch where I hold my arms."

At the end of the afternoon, Steve has knocked over a half second off his time, and the two head for the convenience store for a sports drink.

"So, how's everything else going for you?" Jeff asks as he lifts the bottle and takes a gulp. "What's going on at school?"

"Man, I just don't know," Steve responds. "I guess running isn't the only place I'm having trouble with balance. I'm kind of struggling with a lot of other stuff, too."

"What's going on?" Jeff asks.

Steve, whose grandfather established the church, and whose dad is on the board, attends public school, where he is co-captain of the football team and editor of the yearbook.

"I want to do the right things, and I don't want to let my parents down," Steve says, slowly shaking his head, "but I want to be normal, and fit in with my friends, too. It's getting harder and harder to hang around them and not get caught up in their whole mess."

They leave the store and on the ride home, while picking at the label on the sweating bottle, Steve blurts out, "I just don't see how I'm supposed to live up to everybody's expectations—home, church, and school. I need a better reason to hang on than just being good!"

Quiet for a beat or two, Jeff stops the car and suddenly looks Steve straight in the eye. "Dude!" he says, his voice filled with urgency and excitement. "What if your whole reason for being at that school is so that God can use you as a missionary to the kids on that campus? You're always talking about how sad and messed up the lives of some of your friends are—what if the whole reason you're there is to help them understand that God loves them and wants to help them? If you believed that, then what would you do?"

"I never looked at it that way!" Steve replies.

Jeff says, as he pulls up in front of the house, "Man, you can make a difference in that whole school." "There's no telling what God will do if you let Him!"

Jeff drives away as Steve heads up his front steps, one more young believer strengthened, enabled, and encouraged by the confidence that Jeff has just passed on.

That confidence, which he has given away time and again in the 12 years he has been in ministry, was purposefully built into his life by his mother's words and his father's example.

Jeff is one of three brothers, all of whom are in full-time ministry today. Their dad began in youth ministry and later became senior pastor, and their mom is a pastor's daughter. Yet they never encouraged any of their sons toward choosing careers in ministry.

"In fact, we tried talking them out of ministry," Jeff's mom, Ruth, said.

His dad, Chuck, added, "If you can be talked out of ministry, you're not really called."

"We worked hard at encouraging our sons to be all God wanted them to be, no matter what field they work in, because people can serve God anywhere," Ruth said. "I don't believe we pushed the guys to be music or youth pastors, but simply to serve God because they wanted to."

Jeff believes that his upbringing was the most influential factor in his life and ministry. "The things we did in our home, the daily routines that included our relationship with God and service to others, and the fact that everything revolved around Scripture and music determined my mind-set," he said. "Even if I heard music by Jimi Hendrix or the Beatles, it always played back to my relationship to the Lord and to Scripture."

As he grew, Jeff watched Chuck.

"The greatest heritage I have from my dad is that he was consistently the same person in the pulpit as he was at home. I was glued to what he said, and I never heard him say something that didn't match up with what I saw at home," Jeff said.

"I have a picture in my head of Dad's youth group," he said. "The kids really got what was going on. I saw older kids serving and really engaged. I could tell that they were receiving something. Seeing that—to see that my Dad had that much influence, played into my respect for my Dad's authority."

Jeff watched his father, and he listened to his mother.

"My mom told me every day how awesome I was," Jeff said, "and because of that, I took risks."

On his worst days, Ruth was his biggest cheerleader.

"In high school, our house rules were pretty strict, so we didn't have lots of close friends, but I still believed I could do anything," Jeff said. "My senior year, there were some problems with a lack of leadership at school, and my mom encouraged me to run for student body president."

So Jeff campaigned, never thinking he would really win. But he did.

"She told me all that year, 'You have a voice with people. If you say it, Jeff, they will listen.'"

All of that added up to the effective, dynamic ministry that is Jeff's life today.

"I love to encourage people," he said. "If I see someone struggling, I want to help them make it up the mountain. I love to look kids in the eye and tell them how great they are, to help them understand that they are creatures of God, and He loves them."

"It's my crazy sense of who I am," Jeff said. "I'm never so discouraged by somebody that I don't talk to them. I always think, 'If I could get five more minutes, I'm sure I could reach them.'"

And so with the faith and confidence instilled by his parents, Jeff continues to try.

CHAPTER 9

Planting Seeds and Pulling Weeds

God has given each of you a gift from his great variety of spiritual gifts. Use them well to serve one another.
—1 Peter 4:10 (NLT)

"The maid who sweeps her kitchen is doing the will of God just as much as the monk who prays—not because she may sing a Christian hymn as she sweeps but because God loves clean floors. The Christian shoemaker does his Christian duty not by putting little crosses on the shoes, but by making good shoes, because God is interested in good craftsmanship."—Martin Luther

She had 19 children, and money was often a really big problem. Her husband's job took him out of town so much that the household management was mostly left to her alone. Twice the house had burned to the ground, and illness had taken the lives of several of her infant children. Yet, this godly mother never lost her focus. She determined that each of her children would know God and that she would diligently encourage His calling in each individual child's life.

In the midst of all this turmoil, Susannah Wesley was able to instill in the hearts of her sons John and Charles an unquenchable hunger to follow God and reach out to others with His love. John and Charles often acknowledged that their ministry was a result of what their mother had invested in their lives. And, through their ministry, one of the greatest revivals in the history of the church blossomed during the eighteenth century.

Other than the fact that they lived almost 300 years ago, the Wesley children were not much different from your family today. One church historian said they were "a cluster of bright, vehement, argumentative boys and girls, living by a clean and high code, and on the plainest fare; but drilled to soft tones, to pretty formal courtesies; with learning as an ideal, duty as an atmosphere and fear of God as law." In other words, they were good kids who, even though they were taught to do otherwise, sometimes got way too rambunctious. And with a house as full as the Wesley's, fights were inevitable.

Sound familiar?

So what made the difference? How was Susannah Wesley able to create an atmosphere in her home that would produce John and Charles's passion for their mission? In his personal journals, John revealed his mother's priority as a parent through her own words:

> I cannot but further observe that even she (as well as her father, and grandfather, her husband, and her three sons) had been, in her measure and degree, a preacher of righteousness. This I learned from a letter, written long since to my father, part of which I have here subjoined:

> February 6, 1711–12
> As I am a woman, so I am also mistress of a large family, and though the superior charge of the souls contained in it lies upon you; yet, in your absence, I cannot but look upon every soul you leave under my care as a talent committed to me under a trust by the great Lord of all the families both of heaven and earth. And if I am unfaithful to Him or you in neglecting to improve these talents, how shall I answer unto Him, when He shall command me to render an account of my stewardship?

Susannah brought up a houseful children—individuals uniquely gifted by God, created for His purposes, and called to a particular mission. Her letters reveal that she scheduled her personal attention toward one different child each evening. As large as this household was, it was her responsibility before God to know each child intimately—their abilities and strengths, their weaknesses, their hopes and dreams, and all that was deep in their hearts. She saw in John, the potential to be a fiery preacher and a gifted organizer. Charles was the creative child, and she encouraged his writing and music. Later, he would compose some of the church's most beloved hymns.

> Your child, too, is unique, and is uniquely called.

Your child, too, is unique, and is uniquely called. Whether their mission is to minister to one family, as Susannah Wesley did, or to millions like John and Charles Wesley did—or perhaps to operate a business that can provide financial support for ministry, or to teach a Sunday School class, or simply be a good friend—your job is to recognize the special gifts and strengths in each child's life, and affirm them. Our goal is to encourage them to ask the Father, "What do you want me to do?" From their earliest days, we want to train their eyes to see what God sees, their hearts to respond to what God cares about, and their hands to do God's calling.

One of the most difficult tasks of parenting is helping our children to define who they are. The job calls for delicate balance in which we must be fully committed but yet understand that, ultimately, it's not our choice at all. This is between our child and God. Our tendency is to force them into a mold that we create, so as to streamline the process. That way, they can bypass all the "what ifs," the detours that all of us seem to take in determining God's will for our lives. But is that how God really wants it to happen?

God's plan for parents is that we carefully lead our kids to their own personal discovery about what He created them to be. It's one of those tasks that we don't have the privilege of bringing to a conclusion. Our job is just to set in motion the lifelong process of accurate self-evaluation that is vital to any healthy Christian walk. Paul cautioned believers about how and why God wanted that to happen for all of us.

> *Because of the privilege and authority God has given me, I give each of you this warning: Don't think you are better than you really are. Be honest in your evaluation of yourselves, measuring yourselves by the faith God has given us. Just as our bodies have many parts and each part has a special function, so it is with Christ's body. We are*

many parts of one body, and we all belong to each other.
—Romans 12:3–8 (NLT)

An agricultural analogy works very well here. The earlier in our child's life that we can plant these healthy seeds, the more completely they will be able to experience the fulfillment of living an adventurous life of faith, confident of God's calling. This is one of those times when God wants parents to tend the garden that is our kids' hearts. In this case, we're not directed to be teachers but to be inspirers. Our goal is to encourage them to think about who they are, to discover what God has invested in them, and to find out for themselves what God is calling them to do. We aren't the ones producing the fruit of their mission, because that's between God and our kids. We have to prepare the soil of our children's spirit to receive truth about who they are, and then we have to be diligent to keep the weeds out. You remember those weeds from when you were growing up—the doubts that followed failure, the unkind words from others that cut so deeply, the rejection and the fears. Those are the things that choke out truth about who we really are in Christ and damage your child's capabilities.

Think about how early in life you began to see your new baby's personality developing. After only a few months, babies begin to demonstrate those traits that make them unique. Their natural curiosity about certain sounds, sights and sensations, their sense of humor, their stubbornness or compliance, are all soon evident. As we start to observe their strengths and proclivities, we begin encouraging the positive potential found there. And it continues throughout the time they're growing up.

Self-evaluation requires questions. To help our kids grasp God's work in their lives, we begin the process by asking those questions on their behalf. The accuracy of the evaluation is determined by where we find the answers, and that begins with you and others who know your child the best. Your spouse, grandparents, or aunts and uncles who spend quality time with your child are a great source since they, too, have a vested interest in that life. Begin the discussions with them. The questions aren't complex, but they do require plenty of ongoing discussion and thought.

✔ What are my child's most prominent personality traits?

✔ How could those traits be considered a strength? In what ways could they become a hindrance?

✔ Does my child have any outstanding talents or abilities?

✔ What activities does my child enjoy the most?

Sometimes we need a bit more objective input in our evaluation. It's important to seek out those who have ongoing interaction with our kids but who see them in settings outside the home. Invite their teachers, Sunday School teachers, or your neighbors out for coffee and ask them if they could be involved in your project. Spend some quality one-on-one time with them, and most of them will feel honored that you value their input. Listen to their opinions carefully and consider them honestly. Don't give in to the feeling that you need to defend your child or explain their actions and choices. Sometimes the answers to these questions may be unexpected, occasionally they may be less than accurate but, most often, they provide a perspective that you can't get anywhere else. Ask trusted individuals:

✔ How does my child get along with others?

✔ Do you consider my child to be a leader or more in the background?

✔ What do you see as strengths? Weaknesses?

✔ What talents and abilities does my child display?

TWO SIDES OF THE COIN
Martha's Perspective as a Mother
As we worked with each of our children to develop their natural gifts and abilities, we discovered that each strength could also potentially become a detrimental weakness, left unattended.

As I prayed for my unborn daughter, I found myself praying at what I believe was the direction of the Holy Spirit, that she would have a heart that responded to God and to the needs of others. Sure enough, from earliest childhood, Annie has been quick to respond when she senses

God's direction, quick to sense needs, and quick to offer a prayer or take any measures to meet those needs. However, that sensitivity and compassion tended to also cause her to let emotion lead her in some decisions and relationships. Particularly, as she began to date, we noticed that she was drawn to try to help people who had major problems in life in ways that we thought were not particularly healthy. So we began to pray and to talk with her about the need to seek God's wisdom in such situations. She learned to ask God's direction first, and then to respond, rather than to react.

Today as a teacher at an inner-city school, her compassion and caring open the door for her to minister to her students in ways that change their lives, but she does so with wisdom and godly purpose.

From his earliest moments, I sensed that the description of Joshua in Scripture, as a "strong and mighty man of God" would apply to our son, Matt. Greg and I made it a point to speak that into his life any time an occasion arose, to teach and encourage him to be strong in his faith and courageous in his decisions, choices, and relationships.

But from his toddler days to adulthood, we discovered that the strength of will that God had gifted him with also meant that he could be uncommonly stubborn. It became a challenge for us—and as he grew to his teens, for him—to temper that stubbornness.

Because of God's gifting and purpose for his life, Matt has naturally been a leader, moving from being captain of his football team and Fellowship of Christian Athletes huddle leader in high school to the leadership team, and then a staff position at the church he attended during college. It has been his challenge to ask God to develop in him humility and a servant heart, even as he found himself in places of leadership.

As a high school teacher and church planter today, the strength of his commitment to God and His call inspires his students and his church members, but he leads with patience and consideration that he has had to work to develop in himself.

In seeking to discover and encourage the spiritual gifting of each of our children, we as parents should also be alert to the potential weaknesses and work with our children to develop a wholesome balance, so that our kids may truly become everything that God has designed them to be.

At this point in the process, you've only plowed the field. Now it's time to plant the seeds that will enable your child to be fruitful. With the insight that you've already gained about your child, present the kind of questions to your kids that will lead them into the self-discovery that directs them toward their mission.

✔ What's the one thing that you enjoy doing most?

✔ What do you want to be when you grow up?

✔ When do you feel closest to God?

✔ What do you think you do best?

And now, we have to deal with those weeds. The adventurous spirit of a child can be crushed by unkind words and doubt. Those are simply lies that have to be overcome with truth. These aren't more questions to be asked, but faith-filled facts to be implanted. Fill your kids' hearts and minds with positive expressions of what you know to be true about them.

✔ I've noticed that you're really good at...

✔ God loves you so much, and He has such a great plan for your life.

✔ I want you to know that I'm always here for you.

✔ God made you so special!

These conversations with your kids will change as they grow up, but the purpose and tone remains the same. The details may get more precise, but your child also might become a little more guarded in response to your leading questions. That's the reason that it's very important to begin early, so that you can establish a pattern of communication with them that they become comfortable with. Though a teenager might not answer your questions as freely as little ones do, the infusion of truth that you instill will always be received deep inside their hearts.

Martha's Perspective from Her Childhood

I have to interrupt with another personal story here. I grew up in a west Texas "oil town" in the late 50s. There was an unusual interest in the arts there and, though my father was a machinist and money was tight, my parents went to great lengths to discover what my talent might be.

Like all of the other little girls, at the age of four I started ballet lessons from Miss Jeannie Willingham. Once a week I donned my pink leotard, tights, and ballet slippers, and went to the Knights of Columbus Hall to practice first position, second position, and so on, holding the bar in front of a wall of mirrors that the men had installed, so that Miss Jeannie would pay them rent for their hall.

All was well until the night of the big recital, which nearly everyone in town attended, in the junior high school auditorium.

Dressed in my pink flower petal tutu, I performed with the rest of my age group, going through the motions with as much grace as a four-year-old can muster. Until...

Another girl and I were supposed to make our exit through the back curtain while everyone else danced off to either side. I don't know whether there was something on the floor behind the curtain or I was just clumsy, but I somehow ended up flat on the floor for my final exit.

That night in the car as we drove home, my parents asked me in bright, cheerful voices, "How would you like to take piano lessons?"

Flash-forward one year, to the night of the piano recital when, once again, nearly the entire population of the town had gathered.

I spread the skirt of my frilly taffeta dress across the bench and proceeded to perform my painstakingly memorized recital piece, "The Busy Little Mill Wheel."

Everything was going great until I suddenly realized that I had somehow spaced out, and I had no idea where I was in my piece.

Instead of hitting a chord to signal an end and standing to make my curtsy, I stopped playing, jumped up, covered my mouth and said, "Oops! I think I made a mistake!"

On the way home that night, my parents asked me if I would like to take art lessons.

It's a funny story, but as I look back, I understand that my parents were proactively helping me discover what my God-given abilities might be.

The happy ending to the story is that my ninth-grade English teacher, a lovely, gracious woman named Gladys Batson (who often had to ask me to stop talking!) called me aside one day, to tell me that she thought I was a gifted writer.

"Do you ever write anything other than for class assignments?" she asked me.

"Well, yes. I like to write stories and poems just for fun sometimes," I admitted to her.

"Wonderful! Would you let me read them sometime?" she asked.

And those words of affirmation were the momentum that started me down the road to a degree in journalism and a life fulfilled by serving God at His calling.

Words of encouragement, hope, and promise bless each member of your family. Because we live in a world that daily robs us of those commodities, being intentional about replanting them is a vital mission to which parents have been called. In pointing out to your children the gifts, strengths, and abilities within them, you become God's agent. He created them with all the qualities they need to fulfill the mission He's placed before them, and His desire is that they see themselves as He sees them. As your children discover the depth and the breadth of His investment in their lives, they begin to reach beyond the ordinary. They will boldly pursue their mission!

THINK

▲ When I think of my children serving God, do I think only along lines of church or missions work?

▲ Considering each member of my family, what talents or interests have I observed in each?

▲ Are there actions I could take or words I could speak that would encourage them to develop those abilities?

❏ Ask your children questions about the activities they most enjoy doing and why they like them.

❏ Ask them to list the things they think they are good at. Tell them what you notice. Don't forget that things like being friendly, being helpful, being a good listener, caring for animals, or sharing belongings count!

❏ Then, as a family, think of ways God might use those activities or skills to bless others or bring glory to Himself.

● ● ● ● GOOGLE THIS: ● ● ● ●

✎ Ways to serve God.

✎ Ways to serve others.

✎ Now make your own list!

▬ ▬ ▬ LIVE IT! ▬ ▬ ▬

The little girl holds tightly to her mother's neck, her thick, cropped brown hair tousled and sticking to her chubby cheeks in the steady rain that creates puddles in the muddy street of her Argentine village.

Her brother, an eight-year-old with a quick smile and almond-shaped eyes the color of chocolate syrup, grips his mother's skirt as he shifts his weight from one split, calloused foot to the other in the mud.

Neither child has ever owned a pair of shoes, but today as they stand patiently with their mother in the rain, their eyes are wide with anticipation in their usually passive faces. All of that is about to change.

The American man and his friends are here, and they are giving away shoes.

As the line inches forward, one by one the children are measured, then a smiling young American carefully places a brand-new pair of Tom's Shoes onto their small, often cut and calloused feet, eliciting spontaneous hugs and slow, warm smiles before the children run away to play.

Standing aside for a moment, surveying the scene of the first ever "shoe drop," which is providing 10,000 pairs of shoes to children in poor Argentine villages, Blake Mycoskie is overcome with emotion to see his dream, birthed only 14 months ago, become a reality.

It had begun as a simple vacation to Argentina, to take some polo lessons and relax a bit. At 29, Blake had already been successful at a couple of business ventures and had appeared with his sister as a contestant on the CBS reality series, *The Amazing Race*. By the third week of his vacation, he decided that some volunteer work was in order, so he found himself on an Argentine farm, sitting on the porch at the afternoon break, just observing.

"I had seen the rope-soled canvas shoes, called *alpargatas*, that the workers wore. I bought a pair and wore them on the trip, because they were comfortable," Blake said. "I looked at the canvas shoes and thought, *These could be made really cool, and think they would sell in the US.*"

The fashion scene is always changing, so it was conceivable that the new fresh style could start to catch on. Blake's idea, though, didn't stop at creating a trendsetting design. In a spark of inspiration, he envisioned building a company with a business model even more extraordinary than the product itself.

"I noticed that in Argentina many of the adults and most of the children were without shoes, and many had feet that were hurting as a result. To me, that was a basic need, and I wanted to help. I decided I could start a company that gives away one pair of shoes for every pair sold, keeping it really simple—one for one."

People said it was absurd. Giving away shoes would surely never allow for a healthy bottom line. Blake had totally opted for the nontraditional, even giving himself the title of Chief Shoe-Giver rather than CEO. Business experts said that it would be impossible to operate a company like that. But they never figured in one factor—this was a "God thing."

Now only a little over a year later, his shoes, which he calls "Toms" because he sees them as "shoes for *tomorrow*," are being worn by celebrities and superstars in all the trendy circles. His name and the story of this unheard-of business model has been touted on *Oprah* and in the pages of *Vogue*, *Elle*, and *Time*, and even Blake is amazed at the fashion frenzy. Toms shoes can be found in the chic boutiques of Manhattan, all the exclusive shops on Rodeo Drive in Beverly Hills, and now in the trend-setting fashion houses of Paris. Sales have increased exponentially so, true to the vision, Blake and his staff continue to place a pair of shoes onto the feet of a child for every pair that is sold. And, as the company expands, so does the outreach. Blake plans to distribute more than 60,000 shoes in Africa on his next shoe drop.

The roots of the unique business model, based on giving rather than profit, and the confidence to set about immediately making his dream a reality can be found in the experiences and attitudes of his childhood home.

He watched as his father, a doctor, invested time and care in each of his patients. His mother worked long hours volunteering in the community, yet always made time for creating a close knit family. As the Mycoskies spent time together at home or on treasured family vacations, their values and approach to giving of themselves were adopted by their son.

"My dad is very compassionate to all people and very humble, and my mom has a giving heart and volunteers all the time," Blake said. "They have always lived their lives very selflessly, so I learned to see needs and approach giving that way."

His parents, loving and nurturing, made the decision to allow their kids to make some mistakes as a way to build confidence.

"Growing up, my parents made me believe that I can't fail," Blake said. "Even if I tried something that didn't quite make it, it counted as a learning experience. They always backed me up. I didn't ever have to worry about failing."

While Blake's parents impacted his attitudes and goals, the vibrant faith of his high school tennis coach, Glen Williams, finally convinced him to surrender his life to Christ.

"I was with him an hour every weekday for two years, and he never forced his belief on me, but he influenced me," Blake said. "There was so much joy in his life, and I was drawn to that. I had to know the source of that, and he drew me along in little baby steps."

Because of this, Blake doesn't see himself as a bold evangelist, believing that his actions will speak louder than words.

"You might not even know about my faith until you've known me a few months," he said. "I don't loudly proclaim my Christianity. I like for people to discover it by being around me. I want them to ask me questions."

With the example of his parents' lives and the confidence they instilled in him, added to the depth of his faith, Blake noted a need on that afternoon in Argentina and took it upon himself to find a way to give selflessly.

"I had always thought that I would spend the first part of my life making money and the last part giving it away," he said. "But I realized that you don't have to put giving on hold. It's something Christ did. You build giving into your life from the very beginning. Even as a carpenter, He gave Himself in service every day. Anyone can do that."

There is another picture of Jesus that Blake has deliberately incorporated into each of the shoe drops. Rather than simply delivering a crate of shoes to each village, or even handing a pair of shoes to each of the children there, Blake and his employees model the humility of Christ washing the disciples' feet.

"We won't just pass the shoes out, we get down face-to-face with the kids and put the shoes on their feet," he said. "Otherwise, it's human nature to pat ourselves on the back, congratulate ourselves for the good deeds we're doing and forget that this is not about us, but it's all about the kids and their needs."

"As a believer, I've always had a heart for the sick and the poor, but I've never had an outlet before this," he said.

With his vision for how a basic need for children to have shoes might be met, Blake wasted no time putting his idea to work once he returned to the United States.

"Starting a business from scratch is scary," he admitted. "In my work and in my life, I have just learned to trust that God is there for me. I know He loves me, and His grace is there. I make mistakes. I hit obstacles. But I just persevere because, at the end of the day, there's His grace."

The little boy, proudly sporting a pair of navy blue Toms, runs up and throws his arms around Blake's legs, and Blake drops to one knee to return the hug. Lifting the boy's sister to his shoulders and surrounded by children, each happily clad in a pair of his shoes, he takes off at a joyful gallop down the puddled road.

"It's about giving people love," Blake said. "The shoes are an excuse for coming, but it's really all about these kids."

Then the King will say, "I'm telling the solemn truth: Whenever you did one of these things to someone overlooked or ignored, that was me—you did it to me."
— Matthew 25:40 (*The Message*)

Let It Shine!

CHAPTER 10

Living in the Land of *What If?*

"For nothing is impossible with God."
—Luke 1:37 (NLT)

The beautiful Texas hill country was in full bloom with wildflowers that day. The summer heat hadn't yet overcome them. Our wedding was to take place in just a little over a month, but we had set aside our planning to attend a leadership conference there.

Lloyd Ogilvie, who was pastor of the Hollywood Presbyterian Church in California at that time, was the speaker that day. Later he would serve as the chaplain of the United States Senate, his dynamic, booming voice leading lawmakers to God at the beginning of every session. Any thoughts of our upcoming wedding took a momentary backseat as we listened to Ogilvie. He challenged us with words that we have never forgotten. "What would you do for God if you knew, for certain, He couldn't fail?"

Think about that question for a moment. We readily make the claim about nothing being impossible with God. It's something that's foundational to Judeo-Christian beliefs. Those of us who were brought up in church have heard it since we were toddlers, but a problem arises when we try to translate it from being just words to becoming a personal lifestyle. If we really believe it's true, why is it that most of our decisions are made based on what we think is realistic and doable? If God is really who we say He is, then He actually can do whatever He wants to do. But we can handcuff what He wants to do in and through our lives just because we refuse to dream.

Kids are dreamers. If you think back far enough, you can probably recall what you dreamed about when you were their age. Forbes.com surveyed a kindergarten class about what they wanted to be when they grew up: "Seven out of 33 five-year-olds say they want to be superheroes when they grow up, making it the single most popular career choice for kindergartners. (For the record, Spider-Man was number one.) Three kids want to be princesses, and one hopes to grow up to be SpongeBob SquarePants."

Those are mighty high ambitions! As we mature, we begin to understand that childhood dreams don't often mesh well with reality. So we begin to lay aside our plans and face the way things really are. The death of a dream is difficult and, even as kids, we might carry a little bitterness about it. The saddest part, though, is if we allow our "maturity" to kill not only our dreams, but the dreams of everyone else around us.

In order for our children to become missional, we have to let them have dreams. We need to point them to God and allow Him to bring them through the process of finding their gifting and discovering their calling. We question them, we suggest, we inspire and, then we dream right along with them.

That can be an uncomfortable place for an adult to be, so often we parent with safety nets. We don't want to put God on the spot. If He doesn't come through, how do we explain that? Suppose we get in over our heads? Then what do we do? As a result, we not only protect our family, we try to protect God too. We reason that if we stay slightly noncommittal we can work our way through any mess that might come along. If we leave the back door open, we can escape—if need be.

Tony Campolo is not one to mince words. His forthright honesty is sometimes unpleasant for us to hear, but he presents needful challenges. He has expressed the concern that this generation is losing its freedom and ability to dream courageously.

"Here is what the Bible says, 'And when the young no longer have dreams and the old no longer have visions, people perish.' I spend most of my time on university campuses," Campolo said. "Sometimes it upsets me because as I talk with the children, your children, they have no dreams—they have no visions. Let me tell what you have told them. You told them to be happy. 'Mom, what do you think I ought to be?' Ask any father, any mother. Every mother in America answers the same way. 'I really don't care as long as he is happy.' It kind of makes you puke, doesn't it?"

Being happy won't make your child missional.

Being happy won't challenge them.

Being happy won't help them be strong.

It won't stretch them to reach for greater things. It won't help them learn anything about themselves. Though it might temporarily create a pleasant atmosphere, being happy is not a goal that will bring the results that we really want in our kids.

What do you do when your son loves playing basketball, but he's one of the shorter kids in his second-grade class? In order to keep our son from being disappointed, we tried to divert Matt from his passion for the sport and point him in other directions. He would talk about his goal in life—to be an NBA player—and we would quickly offer alternatives. After all, the genes just weren't on his side. Maybe we were cushioning him from inevitable disappointment, but our tactics were dead wrong.

Bobby Jaklich is now the superintendent of one of the major school districts in the San Antonio area. Quite a few years ago, he was the basketball coach at our local high school, and he appreciated seven-year-old Matt's enthusiasm so much that he made him the ball boy for his team. Maybe it was because Bobby at five feet ten had carved out an impressive college basketball career himself, or maybe it was because he had a son of his own, but he was disturbed when he heard our interaction with Matt. "Don't ever tell him what he *can't* do," Bobby said as he took us aside. "As time goes by he'll figure out his limitations. Then he'll either deal with them and overcome them, or he'll move on to the next place where he can shine."

That became a parenting principle that we employed, far beyond athletic fields and courts, into the venue of their walk with God. It did seem hypocritical that we would, on one hand, tell our kids how God had gifted them, and then not wholeheartedly encourage them to dream big dreams about what they might do with those gifts. Our intention was to keep our kids from being disappointed and to keep God's reputation intact. Thankfully, we began to understand that God could protect Himself. We realized that He is able to refine those childlike dreams, that might seem somewhat like a fantasy, and create from them a bold reality.

What if, instead of being the ones who built walls of limitations in our children's lives, we became the source of more possibilities for them? What if we put aside the "maturity" we've attained and began to allow God to stretch us on behalf of our family? That requires us to have the same faith that a child has. It's not an impossible thing to ask of ourselves. In fact, Jesus said that it was exactly what we are supposed to do.

> *One day some parents brought their children to Jesus so he could touch and bless them. But the disciples scolded the parents for bothering him. When Jesus saw what was happening, he was angry with his disciples. He said to them, "Let the children come to me. Don't stop them! For the Kingdom of God belongs to those who are like these children. I tell you the truth, anyone who doesn't receive the Kingdom of God like a child will never enter it." Then he took the children in his arms and placed his hands on their heads and blessed them.*
> —Mark 10:13–16 (NLT)

It's been so long since some of us have been childlike that it might be hard to remember how it felt. So it's a good thing that God gave us a convenient reminder in the 37th Psalm:

> *Delight yourself in the LORD, and he will give you the desires of your heart. Commit your way to the LORD; trust in him, and he will do this.*
> —Psalm 37:4–5 (NIV)

This is an invitation from God to dream big dreams before Him. It requires a childlike heart, though. If you want to allow your kids to imagine doing great things for God, then not only do you have to let them dream their dreams, you have to dream right along with them. Parents teach their children to dream big things for God when they lead the way. David, a man after God's heart, was childlike in his relationship with God. When he wrote Psalm 37, he presented us with a process of how we, too, could enjoy that kind of connection with our heavenly Father. There are four action words in those verses that demonstrate the purity and beauty of a childlike heart.

Delight. Do you remember the story of when David stripped down to his underwear in front of everyone and danced before God? When we read this portion of Scripture, we're usually just a bit embarrassed on David's behalf, so we move past it pretty quickly. His own wife was even upset with him over the incident. We're not required to imitate David's actions here, but it is very important that we replicate his heart. David took great delight in his relationship with God. That was the primary focus of his life, and he was joyful and unrestrained in his worship. David was an imperfect man, capable of things that were ugly, yet he sought and received God's forgiveness and, in that renewed relationship, he found joy.

Foundational to our childlike faith is that unrestrained joy. Are you having a hard time finding it within yourself? There were times when David did, too. After his adulterous relationship with Bathsheba and the subsequent plot to murder her husband, David was distant from God and separated from His joy. In Psalm 51, he cried out for forgiveness, and the focus of that prayer was that God would restore his joy. In spite of difficult circumstances and our own failures, God remains as the available source of joy in our lives. It's there for us simply by choosing it and asking Him for it. And when we're truly and freely joyful in our home, it's contagious.

Desire. It's not a dirty word—*desire*. And *passion* is not necessarily R-rated. The thing that can make those words distasteful, though, is the object of our desire. Too often, we've probably misinterpreted the object of desire in the context of Psalm 37. God isn't making Himself available as some sort of a vending machine here. This isn't an invitation to drop your "desire" coin in the slot, choose from a multitude of great things that are available, press your selection, and ta-da! it's all yours. Instead, as you delight yourself in the Lord, this is about Him placing the desires in your heart that will bring focus to the mission He has called you to. Those desires are pure and selfless because they're what He's passionate about. They are childlike desires, uncluttered by selfishness and greed.

When God, Himself, becomes the object of our desire, Jesus said that the other concerns of life are placed in proper focus:

> *"So don't worry about these things, saying, 'What will we eat? What will we drink? What will we wear?' These things dominate the thoughts of unbelievers, but your heavenly Father already knows all your needs. Seek the Kingdom of God above all else, and live righteously, and he will give you everything you need."*
> —Matthew 6:31–33 (NLT)

Commit. What does it mean to be committed to something? Because "commitment" is an indefinable commodity, it's impossible to measure it. We do know it when we see it, though.

We live and breathe football in Texas. There are pockets around the country that might come close to rivaling the intensity of Texas football; in this state, it's huge. Football affects the way almost all of us live. It can't be helped, because it's just the nature of things.

There's a story told about a guy who settles into his seat at the Texas high school football championship. The game has been a sell-out for more than a week, but at the end of the first quarter, he notices that there is a seat next to him that's empty. He looks at the man seated on the other side of the empty seat and exclaims, "I'm amazed that this seat is empty. Who would miss a game like this?"

"Oh, that's my wife's seat," the man answered. "We've been to the last 24 Texas state championships, but, sadly, she passed away."

"Oh, that's terrible. I'm so sorry. But couldn't you get a friend or another family member to come to the game with you?"

"No," he said, "they're all at the funeral."

Activities are planned around Texas football; weddings and funerals have had to be rescheduled because of it and, most of the year, it's a regular topic of conversation at work, at church, at school, in the stores and restaurants, and at most family dinner tables.

But, even though most Texans can't escape football's influence, there are some in our state who take it over the top. Open their closets and you'll see a monochromatic collection of apparel that reflects their team's colors. They may even dedicate a room in their home as a shrine for books, posters, banners, pictures, autographs, and an assortment of other unusual products that declare their allegiance. When game day rolls around, they hoist a flag over their house and decorate their vehicles. They cover their faces with war paint and arrive at the stadium as early as possible, grills in tow, to participate in the ritual known as tailgating. Prior to the kickoff, they find their seats that they have reserved for the entire season and begin to yell things that you would never imagine could come from their mouths. These people are definitely *committed*.

Commitment is visible and it's vocal. It's the result of a choice that's been made, so it can't be faked or worked up. Your child will learn commitment to God from what you choose to commit to. That's not easy, because being committed takes a wholehearted effort. There's no wiggle room, no margin for error, and no compromise. It doesn't mean that you have to be perfect in order to model commitment, because that just doesn't happen for any of us. It does mean, though, that there should never be any question about what our intentions and priorities are. That's the kind of commitment that children can understand clearly and follow confidently.

Trust. It's something that kids do much better than adults. In fact, the younger the child, the easier it is for them to trust. That's simply because distrust happens through experience. Every occasion in which we've been hurt, misled, deceived, or taken advantage of, builds that wall of distrust within us. Trust is an attitude seen most purely in the heart of a child. A baby trusts that its needs will be met. But, from the time a child begins to understand that not everyone can be trusted, they head down a path that leads them toward more and more skepticism. Left unchecked and unredeemed, as early as their teenage years, kids may have already developed bitterness and doubt.

How, then, do we regain the childlike quality of trust in our lives? It all begins with the object of our trust. In whom or in what are we trusting? In Psalm 37, God wants us to be certain it really is Him that we're trusting. We can't put our confidence in reason, circumstances, or experiences. All those things shift and, eventually, collapse. They're certain to disappoint us. Just like a child, we can only trust our Father, whose love for us is constant and who never fails us.

Would it help if you had a yardstick that could show you just how you're measuring up in your goal to become more childlike? If you identify with the lyrics of this familiar song, if they touch you and move you, then you're probably headed in the right direction.

Jesus loves me! This I know,
For the Bible tells me so;
Little ones to Him belong;
They are weak, but He is strong.
Yes, Jesus loves me!
Yes, Jesus loves me!
Yes, Jesus loves me!
The Bible tells me so.

"Jesus Loves Me"
Words by Anna B. Warner, Music by William B. Bradbury
(public domain)

Our Father is a God of limitless possibilities, and the ways He can use each person's unique gifts and abilities are unlimited as well. As we lead our children to begin making connections between their giftedness and the ways they might minister to their world, we want to encourage them to dream new, big dreams about how God might lead them toward His purposes.

THINK

▲ Are there hurts or disappointments in my past that might be causing me to "hedge my bets" when it comes to trusting God?

▲ When was the last time I fully put my trust in Him, in spite of circumstances or logic? What happened?

▲ Do I really believe that all things are possible with God? Is there something in my life right now that I need to fully entrust to Him?

DO TRY THIS AT HOME!

❑ Divide the family into pairs. Blindfold one person in each pair. Go on a "trust walk" around the house or yard with the person who can see describing the next step and giving instructions to the one who is blindfolded. Switch places, and do it again. Afterwards, question each other and talk about the difficulties the blindfolded ones had trusting that they weren't going to fall or run into something. As a family, compare those feelings to the ease we have in trusting God.

❑ Share: What is the biggest leap of faith your family has ever made? What happened?

LIVE IT!

Deep in the jungle of Cameroon, West Africa, in the midst of a collection of shuttered mud huts that made up the tribal chief's compound, the moonlight glinted on the windows of the only hut in the village where the shutters were open. The darkness was alive with now-familiar sounds of the night, including the faint whine of mosquitoes. Inside that hut, Pete and Lydia slept in the barely perceptible breeze that floated in through the open window.

Suddenly, the somnolence was shattered by a woman's loud cries and the sound of their shutters slamming shut. Pete and Lydia sprang from their bed in alarm as shutters on their hut banged closed, accompanied by a panicked shout.

"We had arrived among the Messaka people via helicopter at the beginning of the rainy season in 1992, intending to learn the language, Ugar, and then translate the Scripture for them," Lydia explained. "Since Ugar was not yet a written language, we needed to determine the best way to write the sounds, including tones, that would be easy for the people to learn. The best way to facilitate this was to live among the Messaka, so we rented a house in the chief's compound.

"Living next to the chief was good, because we had both his approval for being there, and his protection. The house was a three-room mud block structure with a tin roof," Lydia said. "We had the inside walls and floors covered with cement to help keep it somewhat cleaner, and we put screens on the windows to allow for as much air as possible and still help with mosquito control.

> Pete began to understand what the woman was saying.

"We used solar power to run a small fan, fluorescent lights, and the computer and shortwave radio," she said, describing their life. "We cooked with a propane stove top."

That night, standing in their darkened hut listening to the shouts outside, Pete began to understand what the woman was saying.

"We were a bit alarmed until at last we realized she was trying to protect us from malaria mosquitoes" Lydia said. "Every other house was closed up tight at night to keep the mosquitoes out, but we left our shutters open for ventilation."

The woman had never seen screens on windows before. "We eventually helped her to understand that the screens made it OK to leave the shutters open," Lydia said. "Not until she actually felt the screens did she reopen the shutters."

Such situations made the couple more deeply aware that even simple home improvements were beyond the means of most of their neighbors.

Lydia recalls that the journey that brought her to that night in Africa began in her childhood, with inspiration from an unlikely source.

As an eight-year-old, she had listened to an album by the Singing Nun, and read her story of going to Africa as a missionary. From something as simple as an album cover, a desire was born in her heart to do the same thing.

"It was not until ten years later that I even became a Christian, but I believe that God had planted that desire, and allowed it to grow over the years, until the dream was a reality," Lydia said.

But it did not happen overnight.

"Though we didn't know each other, Pete and I had both attended the same missions conference in 1984, where one of the speakers described the work of Wycliffe Bible Translators. Her talk struck a chord with me," Lydia said, "and I was off and running."

Wasting no time, she began to research the possibility of joining Wycliffe, and though she had to wait and work three years to pay off her financial obligations from nursing school, Lydia often went on short-term medical missions to Mexico.

Meanwhile, God was nurturing a similar dream in Pete's heart, leading him to apply to Wycliffe as well.

In January of 1988, Lydia began her linguistics training at Wycliffe's medical and technical facility in Dallas. Though the work was graduate level and difficult at times, she found it fascinating. And it was there that she met Pete, and they fell in love.

After serving in Africa several years, Pete contracted malaria, and his health eventually was threatened to the point that the couple had to return to the United States.

"It was with mixed feelings that we came home from Cameroon," Lydia said. "On one hand, I felt like the dream had been realized—we had actually gone to Africa as missionaries. But there was also a feeling of failure, since we had come home without intending to return, and the job was nowhere near done. But we've since heard that others have continued the translation work."

———

On a sunny afternoon 15 years after their return, Lydia sat on the couch in her den with her five children, Peter, 11; Julianne, 9; John, 7; Daniel, 6; and Gloria, 4, clustered on the floor around her. They had finished their homeschool lessons, and Julianne had taken the old photo album off the shelf. The kids were pouring over the photos, asking questions, as they had many times before.

"Is that one there the chief?" Julianne asked.

"Let me see!" John said, pulling the book closer.

"No, I want to see," Daniel demanded, giving it a brisk tug toward himself.

"I was looking first!" Julianne asserted, her voice becoming louder.

"Guys!" Lydia intervened. "Daniel, John, is that a good way to show you love each other?"

"No, Mom," the boys answered with downcast gazes.

"And Julianne," Lydia continued, "how would you feel if Peter was talking about the book, but he wouldn't let you see the pictures?"

"I'm sorry, boys," Julianne said.

"How about if we watch the video, and then we can all see it?" Peter, acting as elder statesman, asked and moved toward the shelf to get it.

As Peter popped the video into the player, Pete emerged from his home office.

Dropping onto the couch beside his wife, he gathered Gloria onto his lap as the video transported them back to their missions field.

"There's Mommy in the kitchen!" Daniel pointed. "What food could you cook on that little stove?"

"You didn't ever get pizza, did you?" John piped in.

"Fast-forward to the Namaan the leper song, please, please," Gloria asked. "I want to sing it with them, like we always do!"

As he held down the fast forward button, Peter glanced at his parents and asked a new question.

"Were Grampa and Granny and Mamaw and Pop sad when you went away from them? Would you be sad if I went there someday, too?"

"Yes, honey, they were very sad," Lydia answered, recalling how she and Pete had struggled with a lack of support from both sets of parents.

"We would miss you," Pete said, "but we want you to do whatever Jesus asks you to do when you grow up. There are lots of people here, and everywhere, who need to know Him, so you can tell about Him wherever He wants you to go."

Thinking back on interactions with her children and their time on the missions field itself, Lydia said, "I think we have not told our children about all the hard things we experienced, because we want them to see missions in a positive light. We didn't receive much encouragement from our families when we went to Africa, so we know we don't want our children to have that experience. If any of them felt called toward foreign missions, we would support and encourage them wholeheartedly."

Pete and Lydia hope there will still be a time when their whole family can experience foreign missions together.

"We still have a heart for foreign missions ourselves, and we hope to serve overseas again someday," Lydia said. "We hope it will be before our children are too much older, so that we can have the experience together as a family."

Both Pete and Lydia had short-term missions experiences in cross-cultural settings that helped fuel their desire for long-term service. "We would gladly allow any of our children to try a short-term mission so they could discern if this is a direction the Lord is leading them," Lydia said.

The couple doesn't expect that their children must follow in their footsteps, but they are intentional in cultivating the heart of each child to love God and care about people.

"We ask our children the same questions every night," Lydia said. "'What's the most important thing?' The answer, 'To love God.' And, 'What two things should you obey?' 'Love God and love people.'"

The conversation carries over into their daily family life.

"Sometimes we talk about what it means to love people, especially when we see a lack of love among the children during the day," Lydia said. "We ask questions like, How would you feel if…? or Was that a good way to show someone you love them? These teachable moments come up all the time and in lots of different places, so we stop and ask at the time, while the lesson is fresh and the opportunity presents itself."

As they consider the possibility of foreign missions in the future, Pete and Lydia try to be prayerfully sensitive to the gifts, the personalities, and the needs of each of their children.

"At this point, only one of our children seems to have an interest in missions or outreach," Lydia said. "Julianne will often think out loud about whether or not her friends are saved, and how she could tell them about Jesus or invite them to church.

"She seems to be the most missional of our children. Also, she's the most open to change, like living somewhere else in order to be involved in missions," Lydia said.

"Daniel and Gloria have not expressed an interest one way or another, although Daniel is the most outgoing, and easily makes new friends," she explained. "Peter and John are most concerned about status quo—no major changes and always having home to come back to. I think we'll have to keep this in mind when or if we serve overseas."

Though they are living now far from that tribe in Africa where they began their mission as Bible translators, Pete and Lydia have actually continued their mission in a way they never anticipated. Pete develops fonts, software, and keyboards for multilingual computing, something that can assist the work of Bible translators everywhere, as they also work to raise children whose hearts are open to God.

From living in a hut in Africa, to developing software and home schooling their children, to remaining prayerful about what the future may hold for them or their children, Pete and Lydia strive to model the lesson they are teaching their family: The most important thing, no matter where you are, is to love God and love people.

———

Update: Within months of giving this interview, Pete and Lydia received the phone call they had been hoping for. The entire family took Chinese lessons, sold all their belongings, and boarded a plane for China, where today they are all serving as "house family" at an orphanage.

CHAPTER 11

God's Imagineer

Now these are the gifts Christ gave to the church: the apostles, the prophets, the evangelists, and the pastors and teachers. Their responsibility is to equip God's people to do his work and build up the church, the body of Christ.
—Ephesians 4:11–12 (NLT)

McNair Wilson helps make dreams come true. Anyone who has wandered wide-eyed through one of the Disney theme parks has experienced the magic he and his fellow dreamweavers have created. McNair was a senior imagineer for the Disney Corporation. The term *imagineer* itself is Disney creativity unleashed upon the English vocabulary. It's the title given to the talented members of the engineering and production staff that create and design, among other wonders, attractions at the theme parks. They are the people who bring life to the fantasies of kids and, if we're honest, adults too, as we drink in what lies around every corner of the park.

McNair is a gifted designer, communicator, and producer, blessed with a unique ability to close his eyes, imagine something entertaining, and then create it for others to enjoy. People like him impress us, and we're amazed at what he's able to do. Just what is his deep, dark secret?

He does have a secret, but he really doesn't hold on to it very tightly. Actually, all you have to do is ask him, and he'll gladly share with you all the details. His mission, in fact, is to tell the whole world about it. McNair now communicates his message from pulpits, around executive conference tables, on theatre stages, and even in isolated jungles in Africa, as the experience manager for Compassion International.

His goal is to help people "recapture, harness and pursue" their inherent creativity for the purpose of reaching out to others.

"Our creative spirit, natural curiosity, and sense of wonder are all factory installed," he said. "They might be a bit rusty, dusty, and atrophied, but not lost."

We've emphasized in this book all the hard work that's necessary in order to raise a family of world changers. Those refinery-type tasks are difficult and tedious, but they're necessary if we want our children to seek God's calling for their lives.

Now let's take a look at how we can involve our creative instincts in the process. Being creative isn't always easy, and it's even more difficult for some parents than it is for others. It is, however, the aspect of the parenting job in which we can see more obvious results. We have the opportunity here to observe our kids' responses, and watch the excitement in their eyes when something connects within them. This is our opportunity to be like McNair and those other Disney imagineers when we create experiences for our kids that allow them to taste the variety of flavors that a missional life has to offer.

Imagination and creativity are contagious. When we think outside the box with our kids, they learn the value of it, as well as the richness it brings. And these are the life experiences that stimulate their own creativity, broaden their scope of possibilities, and equip them for the work of serving others.

The Home Experience

It all begins at home. A child's desire to follow God's calling finds deep roots in a home's fertile ground where reaching out to others is a priority.

Life pressures us to build our home into some kind of fortress. The comfortable thing is to make it quiet and isolated from all the nonsense we face throughout the day. The nice thing is to make our home a refuge where just our family can come together to find peace. Sometimes we do need that, and we should be intentional about arranging it—sometimes. But God's ultimate goals for our home are quite a bit different. His Word leaves little question about what should be the atmosphere there.

> *Cheerfully share your home with those who need a meal or a place to stay.*
> —1 Peter 4:9 (NLT)

> *Don't forget to show hospitality to strangers, for some who have done this have entertained angels without realizing it!*
> —Hebrews 13:2 (NLT)

> *Share with God's people who are in need. Practice hospitality.*
> —Romans 12:13 (NIV)

Our home has always been loud and busy. From the time they were just starting school, we eagerly encouraged Annie and Matt to invite their friends over, deciding that it was better to keep an eye on all of them at our place than wonder what was going on at someone else's. By the time our kids were teenagers, we never knew what combination of visitors we would have at our house. One morning, we woke to find Matt's teammates, an entire offensive line including a couple of tackles that weighed in at over 300 pounds, piled into sleeping bags on our living room floor. It was shocking the first time, but we got used to it.

Sometimes it was inconvenient, and we had to learn to wander around the house only if we were dressed decently. It could have become frustrating because we rarely saw any immediate dramatic spiritual impact from it. But several years later in one week, two of our kids' friends, now adults, each sought us out to tell us that our home had provided safety and peace for them. Now we see our own children establishing homes and lifestyles that are focused on ministering to others, being open to those who are in need. That makes it worth any inconvenience we had to put up with.

The Education Experience

Educational issues have become a powder keg, producing controversy and spirited discussion almost every time the subject has arisen. The how and where about a child's education may continue to be a source of disagreement, but there remain some constants about the goals to be achieved. Parents are the greatest influence in constructing their children's attitude about their education. And this attitude, in turn, formulates within each child a clear perspective of not only their future mission, but of their purpose in the present. How can we create an atmosphere where that flourishes? What are the elements of the kind of attitude that our kids should have about education?

It's bigger than the basics. Reading, writing, and arithmetic are skills that must be mastered, but as goals, they're somewhat puny. Most kids can't translate the three Rs into a life challenge that will motivate them to become world changers. So it's important that they understand math is more than just equations and English is greater than nouns and verbs. Education is the search for truth. And truth is found in the beauty and the order of God's world and how He wants us to interact with others.

> The earth is the Lord's, and everything in it.
>> The world and all its people belong to him.
> For he laid the earth's foundation on the seas
>> and built it on the ocean depths.
> Who may climb the mountain of the Lord?
>> Who may stand in his holy place?
> Only those whose hands and hearts are pure,
>> who do not worship idols
>> and never tell lies.
> They will receive the Lord's blessing
>> and have a right relationship with God their savior.
> Such people may seek you
>> and worship in your presence, O God of Jacob.
> —Psalm 24:1–6 NLT

Education has an eternal impact, because God's work in each of our lives is much bigger than the span of a lifetime within the boundaries of a tiny part of the world. What our kids learn, what they know, and what they experience expand the possibilities of how God can use their lives.

It's how you glorify God. It's usually pretty easy for a child to know when they've missed the mark. When they were very small, we used to talk to our kids about how their disobedience had "made God sad." Their response to that was genuine remorse and a desire to make things right again. It's much more difficult, however, for children to comprehend what actions actually bring glory to God. Hard work that produces results is an element of education that they can experience and understand. And that brings glory to God!

Work hard so you can present yourself to God and receive his approval. Be a good worker, one who does not need to be ashamed and who correctly explains the word of truth.
—2 Timothy 2:15 (NLT)

When our son was in third grade, he made a halfhearted attempt at making a poster illustrating the water cycle. It was messy and uninspired and we called him on it. It was C work, at best, and Matt was capable of doing much better. We displayed the poster right there at the kitchen table as a deterrent and insisted that he redo it, correctly this time. He was missing some of his favorite television shows, and he wasn't happy about it. With a little bit of urging, he thought through what would make a good poster and put together the new one, complete with computer-generated labels and a blue cellophane pond. He didn't get to watch television that evening, but when he compared his new poster to the old one, a big smile spread across his face. He was rightfully proud of it, and he was justified because he made an A. And more importantly, we made certain that he knew that his best work brought glory to the God he loved and who loved him. That incident changed the way Matt approached his schoolwork from that day on. Even through graduate school, he would refer to "another water poster experience" when hard work paid off. Matt teaches high school English now, and the story of the water poster has already made it into his instruction to his classes about diligence.

> There are lives in your kids' world that only they can reach.

It doesn't matter whether your children are in public school, in private school or are homeschooled, their calling is to be salt and light there. Sometimes it's difficult for parents to view it from that perspective, but there are lives in your kids' world that only they can reach. Help your child to notice others around him. Talk with her about what she can do to change her world.

We were able to see it happen through our kids' lives. When they were in a public school with a somewhat rough reputation, we watched God work through Anne and Matt in the lives of many students there. Forgive us for boasting a bit about how great our kids were. Well, truthfully, we were as surprised and amazed as anyone at the things God did through their lives. We knew that they were a gift from God, though, and we simply offered them back to Him. And He, in turn, used them in awesome ways.

Through our own children, God taught us something that we've passed on to other parents every time we get the opportunity. He appoints kids to be missionaries on their campuses and to wherever their world extends. We learned that we're not preparing our kids for "someday." We're equipping them for "right now."

The Church Experience

"I don't think I really have to go to church in order to have a relationship with Christ." We've heard that a lot and, technically, that could possibly be correct. But without church, in whatever form gathering with others of like faith takes on in today's culture, it is impossible for us to see ourselves in relationship with other believers. One of the New Testament's prominent themes is how we fit in with others in order for us to maximize the impact of the gospel on the rest of the world. That theme describes our place there, our activity there, and our conduct there.

If our children learn from us that church is a production that we attend on Sunday mornings, then we've totally missed the point, as parents and as a church. The weakest, most ineffective, most destructive concept of church is that we somehow have the option of passing judgment on the music, the sermon, or how comfortable we were. Like modern-day Roman emperors, we offer thumbs-up or, God forbid, thumbs-down on the performance of the Christians that day. If we get bored at this arena, there's another one right down the street. We can just take our business elsewhere.

Joining a church is nothing like buying a ticket to a play or a concert. It obligates us to much more than a seat in the pew. In becoming a part of a church, we are committing our talents and our resources to other people. It's the place where we give and receive strength and reinforcement to serve others within our fellowship, in our community, and around the world.

Your kids will most likely reach a phase where they'll tell you they don't want to go to church. There are a lot of reasons why they'll take this position but, believe it or not, very few of those reasons have anything to do with church at all. It's about who has the upper hand. So this is where you become the imagineer—only with a twist. There are some rides at Disney parks that are really scary, especially if you've never been on them. Once you reassure your kids that everything will be just fine, with just a little insistence, they'll get on the ride. OK, sometimes it may take more than just a little insistence. But once they're there and involved, they'll forget they ever hesitated.

The very same thing happens with your child and church. They'll offer a lot of reasons why they shouldn't go, but stick to your guns, Sheriff. First, you have to know that you can't be hypocritical about this. If you aren't fully immersed in your church and its ministry, no words will convince your kids that it's really important for them to be there. Your complaining about the preacher and his sermons, or the music, or the people, only gives your children carte blanche to voice their own protests. When your own priorities are in order and you are wholeheartedly involved, you have the moral authority to require their participation in the church and its ministries. So be tough and hold your ground on this one—in love, of course!

Now that you're committed to this, you have to be prepared for what you'll face. No need to fear, kids' complaints aren't very original. All of us parents who have gone before you have heard them. Your responses and actions will create the church experience that produces a fruitful believer.

> *The Excuse:* "It's boring."
> *The Response:* "Church isn't about our being entertained. It's about serving and loving others when we're there. That's why we go to Sunday School or youth group. You're there to be an encouragement to your friends."

> *The Excuse:* "But I don't have any friends there."
> *The Response:* "Well, I guess we'll have to help you do something about that. What if you invite several of them out for ice cream after the service? We'll load up the car and take all of you. Better yet, let's just plan a party for the whole group here at the house."

> *The Excuse:* "There's nothing for me to do there."
> *The Response:* "Why don't we talk to your youth pastor and find out where you're needed? You're really talented. I'm sure there will be a place there for you to serve others."

We've seen some beautiful ways that people have served their church. It didn't require any outstanding talents, just a desire to be a part of sharing life with others.

At University Baptist Church in Waco, Texas, where about 1,000 college students make up about 80 percent of the congregation, anyone and everyone is invited to get involved on the Clean Team. UBC doesn't need a paid church custodian because, every Saturday, the Clean Team gets to work, cleaning and preparing the church for the week's services and activities. True servants are developed there who go on to leadership positions in the church. Being involved there weekly, outside the formal gatherings, creates a time of fellowship, meeting people and serving others.

We arrived early for the Sunday morning service at New Christ Memorial Church in San Fernando, California, and watched an elderly woman carefully and lovingly prepare the platform for the service. She straightened the chairs, cleared away any disarray, then she arranged a pitcher of water and drinking glasses on a table where the pastoral staff sat. Pastor Andrae Crouch told us that years before, the woman had come to him and asked how she could serve in the church. "I thought for a moment. Then I told her I get really thirsty while I'm up there preaching," he said. "The very next Sunday she brought the water and glasses for me." She has faithfully fulfilled that calling since then.

These are examples of the type of opportunities that will challenge your kids. And as a result, church will become meaningful and memorable in their lives. That's the church experience we want to create for our children.

The Social Experience

In this culture, broadening our children's social experience is becoming a vitally important aspect of a missional perspective and lifestyle. The inevitable fact of life is that technology has created a world that is shrinking daily. Communities that are made up of people who look alike, think alike, believe alike and act alike are rapidly becoming extinct.

Insulating our kids from other influences will become increasingly more difficult to do. And that may actually be a good thing, because the Scriptures never tell us that's a priority or even a consideration. We're commanded to go and be His witnesses— "in Jerusalem, and in all Judaea, and in Samaria, and unto the uttermost part of the earth." Jesus was criticized within the religious circles because He rubbed shoulders with people who weren't at all like Him.

The social experience we create for our children should include people who are different than we are. They should know people who are a different color, who speak a different language, and who hold different beliefs. Their exposure to "different" helps alleviate any fear they might have of others or any misunderstanding about what others may embrace.

But won't that water down our own experience and faith? Not when the goal is to model Christ to others. Our mission becomes our challenge. We should understand that we are unique, just as others are unique. Our calling is to follow Christ and to love others, so our priorities will necessarily be different.

> They [unbelievers] stumble because they do not obey God's word, and so they meet the fate that was planned for them. But you are not like that, for you are a chosen people. You are royal priests, a holy nation, God's very own possession. As a result, you can show others the goodness of God, for he called you out of the darkness into his wonderful light. Once you had no identity as a people; now you are God's people. Once you received no mercy; now you have received God's mercy.
> —1 Peter 2:8–10 (NLT)

The Serving Experience

Sending your kids on missions trips with their youth group is a great start, but that's only the beginning. For them to not only understand, but embrace a missional lifestyle, serving has to become a part of your child's nature.

Take heart. This may not be as big a challenge as you might expect. In their book *Millennials Rising: The Next Great Generation*, William Strauss and Neil Howe have detected a trend in the attitudes of kids today. They are growing up in the midst of a new cultural sensitivity. As every generation has done, this one is rebelling against what they've perceived as a failure in their parents' lifestyles. They are replacing materialistic, me-first attitudes with social awareness and responsibility. This generation is intent on becoming what, deep down inside us, we knew we should have become. Pop culture gives us some pretty obvious clues about these trends. Study the advertising you see, as companies strive to convince us of their philanthropic awareness. Movies and television programs point out needs around the world and feature feel-good stories of people who are doing something about them.

This offers parents a rare opportunity, that chance to be cool and cutting-edge! Create an atmosphere of giving and serving in your home. The valuable by-product is that, in doing so, you model a missional lifestyle. The opportunities are endless and all around you. Contact missionaries that your church supports, and get in touch with local social assistance organizations. And don't just talk about what the needs are—do something about them! Get involved in service projects with your entire family. As an imagineer who serves, you're able to create vivid scenarios for your kids to experience, while touching lives in your community and around the world.

As our children grow and move into their teen and young adult years, we want to encourage them to express their hearts and their sense of calling. That means we have to listen. It's rewarding, as it becomes our privilege as parents to help them give their dreams feet. It's not always words and counsel that are our most effective tools to assist in this. Behind the scenes, we're creating those experiences that demonstrate how to walk in God's calling. We're working to build a foundation that enables them, helping them get the necessary education, exploring opportunities for them, clearing pathways and making contacts that can move them from being God's dreamers to being God's doers.

THINK

▲ Do I actively look for things to do for God and other people from day to day and week to week?

▲ Are there ways for my children to be exercising their gifts and serving God where they are right now?

▲ What are some experiences in serving that I could create for my family this week?

▲ How does my example of church membership speak to my family about being a "doer of the Word"?

DO TRY THIS AT HOME!

❏ Check the list of service opportunities in your church, and try to identify a place where your family members' talents would be useful. Sign up to serve in that spot for a season. If that's not possible, then select a place where each member's presence and support is needed, and commit to faithful attendance.

❏ Research to see if there is a missions opportunity that would involve your entire family, from youngest to oldest, somewhere in your community.

● ● ● ● GOOGLE THIS: ● ● ● ●

✎ Family mission experiences

▓ ▓ ▓ LIVE IT! ▓ ▓ ▓

"Samuel, you're hearing things," the aged priest said. "Go back to bed. You have a lot of work to do around the temple tomorrow. You need your rest."

Actually, it was Eli who needed sleep. Samuel was too young and energetic to understand how much rest an old man needed. For the second time that night, the boy had come into Eli's room thinking that he had called for him. What an imagination!

Eli had just settled back into bed and had begun to drift off when, once again, Samuel startled him. "Here I am! You called me again."

Eli, now wide awake, was getting angry with the boy. What was this—some kind of game that Samuel was playing? "Learning good manners needs to be on Samuel's agenda," Eli thought.

Just as he was about to chastise the boy, Eli looked into Samuel's face and checked himself. There was something in the boy's eyes that he had seen before. It was not mischief or fear that had brought him into the priest's quarters. This was something deep and real that he could see in his face. It was a divine calling. Samuel was in the midst of an extraordinary experience with God and, by His grace, God was allowing Eli to share a part of it.

Eli had always anticipated that something glorious would happen in Samuel's life. He knew that God had set the boy apart for a unique purpose. It wasn't just random fate. Eli recalled the history that he had with Elkanah and Hannah, the boy's parents. He had recognized that they were godly people, faithful to the Hebrew laws and traditions. But, there was a passion in those people's lives that even superseded their faithfulness. He remembered walking into the temple one day, seeing Hannah travailing in prayer. She was so lost in her communing with God that Eli assumed that she had had a little too much wine. Hannah explained to Eli that she had not had a drop to drink. She was desperate, and she knew that God was her only hope. She wanted a child so badly. There was an emptiness in her life, as if there was something that God desired for her that she had been unable to see come to fruition. Eli saw that passion in her eyes, the intensity of the expression on her face. He was moved by it and spoke a word of blessing over her.

That's the same passionate look that he saw in young Samuel's eyes tonight. He recognized that God was at work deep within the boy's soul, calling from him, personally, a fresh commitment and dedication. As Samuel stood there before him that night, Eli realized that he was responsible to guide the boy through this crucial moment in time. God had been preparing not only Samuel for this moment, but Eli too. It was the reason that Samuel's parents had entrusted the boy's life into the priest's care.

"Samuel, that's God speaking to you. Go back to your room, and when you hear his voice again, just make yourself available to Him. Tell him, 'Speak to me, Lord. I'm listening.'"

Eli placed his hand on the boy's head and spoke a silent blessing over him. He realized that his relationship with Samuel had turned a corner at that moment. During these past few years, Eli had been diligent about connecting Samuel to God. He wanted to show the boy the blessing and reality of serving God and walking in His ways. Samuel had become almost like a grandson to him. And with the unrighteous course his own sons had taken, Eli had rediscovered joy in seeing Samuel's hunger for the things of God. He had seen the boy's faith growing and maturing.

He began to recall all his discussions with Samuel, hoping that he had said the right things. Eli sat straight up in his bed and began to cry out to God. He prayed that Samuel would continue securely on a path toward the Lord. He spoke words of faith, that God would use the truth planted in Samuel's heart to lead him into his calling. (Based on 1 Samuel 3)

CHAPTER 12

Still, Small, and Totally Familiar

He who belongs to God hears what God says.
—John 8:47 (NIV)

"We cover our deep ignorance with words, but we are ashamed to wonder, we are afraid to whisper 'mystery.'"
—A. W. Tozer, *The Knowledge of the Holy*

One of the greatest blessings of our lives is that, for over 30 years, we've had the privilege of spending a lot of time with teenagers. We especially love doing summer camps and retreats with them. We're proud to say that we can still keep up with all the crazy stuff that goes on while we're there but, now that we're older, our recovery time takes a bit longer. There's one thing that has never changed during all those years. When you break through all the activity and noise, you'll find in kids people that hunger for God and really want to please Him. Whenever we talk with a group, there will inevitably be some kids who want to ask us the one important question that they've been dwelling on. They want to know what their next step should be, what the future holds for them. They want to make the right decisions. They want to hear from God.

It's a very natural step in the maturation process. By the time your children reach their high school years, they will begin to get a little sniff of reality. And that starts them thinking. That process begins to reveal itself in various ways. Sometimes they have honest questions, and it motivates them to draw closer to God. Sometimes that thinking leads to questions that lead to even more questions—or to rebellion. But in almost every case, their reactions are based on uncertainty about their future. And even though it can be hidden deep inside them, they're probably fearful or anxious. It's actually a cry out to God for help.

Even good teens get confused. You can be certain that these same questions will at some point be going through your children's heads, even if they haven't expressed them to you yet. Rather intimidating, right? How do you lead them through this? You might feel a need to file this away in that vault that contains such childhood conundrums as "How are babies made?" and "Is there really a Santa Claus?" But this is much more crucial because the course of your child's life might depend on it. There's no need for panic though, if questions manifest themselves in strange ways in your kids. It will simply require patience, honesty, and openness in order to provide the answers that they need to hear.

"Hearing from God" is not an exact science. To begin with, there isn't a specific definition as to what it means. It's not a formula with steps to be followed in order to bring about guaranteed success. Everybody has thoughts about it, and their thoughts are usually based on their own unique experiences. Although there are some basic principles that must be observed for us to confirm God's truth, there is also a lot of unknown territory.

One thing that seems troubling to most people is the terminology itself. When we talk about "hearing," it's generally in the context of the physical exercise of one of our senses. But that's not really what we have in mind when we want to "hear from God."

In order to get a full perspective on this, we turned to some of our family and friends, people just like you, to offer their perspectives and experiences on the subject and help us write this important chapter. These are folks who love God and follow Him wholeheartedly. Although their thoughts shared some similarities, they were different in some ways too. But their wisdom expressed here provides us with a great foundation to build on.

———

Let It Shine!

Matt: "I have never 'heard' from God in the technical sense. God has never manipulated his vocal chords through the exhale of breath, and used his lips, teeth, and tongue to create sounds in a way that created a word (or set of vibrations) that came from 'the heavens' and were received into my inner ear from my outer ear. Do I think this ever happens? Sure. Maybe. I don't know.

"When we talk about 'hearing from God,' I believe we mean that there are things that God wants us to do and doesn't want us to do, in general. We might arrive at it from God's Word, what others tell us, our general feeling about a situation, or a thought deduced using the very functional and capable brains that God gave us to use and make decisions within our following Christ.

"But, it comes down, for me, to this—when we talk about hearing from God, we should talk in terms of experiencing God's presence rather than demanding God's answer. This is much more pragmatic, and much more authentic for me, and just as real as if I had heard a voice. And when we're talking to kids about hearing from God, I think we should dispel myths and undue expectations. We should free them to authentically encounter the living, mighty God, whose presence we intimately feel while His ways we authentically awe and wonder at. This seems like a much healthier approach, as well as an approach that I feel most matches with the character of God as portrayed in Scripture and the character of Christ."

> "We should dispel myths and undue expectations. We should free them."

———

Virtually everyone agreed that the starting point should be searching the Scriptures. God will never tell us something different from what He has already established as truth in His Word.

Jill: "There were times that I wished my parents would just tell me stuff so I could 'move on' with my life (at age 16!). Instead, I was always looking for what God had to say about what I wanted to do. It didn't matter if I was trying to figure out which boy to date, which party to go to, what classes to take, or where I would go to college, my parents would always, without fail, take me to God's Word first.

Sometimes, we can get so caught up in what we're supposed to do next that we neglect another important aspect of the equation. We want God to tell us where we should go next, when He may be more concerned with how we get there.

Scott: "Psalm 37:23 (KJV) says, 'The steps of a good man are ordered by the LORD: and he delighteth in his way.' I see this as the key because, if I understand it correctly, 'who you are' is more important than 'what you do.' With that said, what if, when a major decision faced you, instead of conducting an opinion poll of friends, family, or even 'spiritual leaders', you asked those important people in your life to check your heart? What if, in these moments, we asked those people in our lives to be very honest about all they saw in us? And what if we were committed to responding, examining ourselves, changing wrong attitudes, and repenting. What if instead of asking for advice on what to do, we asked advice on what to become?"

———

When our children were small, their favorite song was "Patience" from Agapeland's *Music Machine* recording, a very creative look at the fruit of the Spirit just for kids. In the song, Herbert the Snail admonished us that sometimes God's timing is not the same as ours. As we seek to know His heart, that's a difficult lesson for any of us, young or old, to learn.

Ruth: "I grew up in a family that desperately depended on God. We prayed for everything—provision, direction, and wisdom. If you were troubled by something, or had a problem, you made an altar—at home if not at church—and prayed until you found peace about the situation. We didn't have instant everything back then. We believed that things that were worthwhile could be waited on."

———

There are many facets to this thing that, as believers, we feel is very foundational to the way we live our lives—we want to hear what God has to say to us and to do what He wants us to do. If adults grapple with the details of it, how are we going to bring it down to the basics for our kids when they first begin to be concerned about it?

You may be significantly stressed out now as you've thought about this vital role that's before you. But don't be. It could very well be that we're just making it all more difficult than it needs to be. The process of hearing what God has to say may be more organic than we make it, a more natural product of following Him in obedience. A. W. Tozer, the noted pastor and writer, was a deep thinker. Many times, his theological discourses were complex. When it came to the discussion of following God's will though, Tozer's advice was to take the simpler, more joyful approach:

> Now, a happy truth too often overlooked in our anxious search for God's will is that in the majority of decisions touching our lives, God expresses no choice, but allows us to choose our preference. Some Christians walk uncertainly, worrying about which profession they should enter, which car they should drive, which school they should attend, where they should live and other such matters. The Lord has set Christians to follow their own personal bent, guided only by their love for Him and their fellow men.
>
> It appears more spiritual to seek God's leading than to do the obvious thing. But it is not. If God gave you a watch, would you honor Him more by asking Him for the time of day or by consulting the watch?
>
> Except for those things that are specifically commanded or forbidden, it is God's will that we be free to choose. The shepherd leads the sheep but he does not decide which tuft of grass the sheep shall nibble. Touching our life on earth, God is pleased when we are pleased. He wills that we be as free as birds to soar and sing our Maker's praises without anxiety. God's choice for us may be any one of a score of possible choices. The Christian who is wholly and joyously surrendered to Christ cannot make a wrong choice."

Tozer knew that this issue created much stress and worry in Christians' lives, so he chose to relieve the pressure. That's a good thing. Your children will grow up hearing many voices demanding to be heard, many opinions pushing to be validated. And there are times that, as their parent, you have to be loud enough to be heard over the din. But sometimes, you have the opportunity to take a different approach. When your children reach an impasse concerning God's wisdom for their lives, your inclination will almost always be to say, very emphatically, "I believe God is trying to tell you..." You might, indeed, have the right answer. But do you trust God's work in your children's lives enough that you can allow them to hear Him for themselves?

Our daughter Annie was a typical middle-school girl dealing with all the issues that middle-school girls deal with. One of her friends invited her to go to her first secular music concert, and Annie was flummoxed. We had always monitored our kids' music quite strenuously. We didn't restrict them to only Christian music, but all the music they listened to was held to a precise standard. The concert was by the "teenybopper" pop group of the day. We considered the music reasonably safe for consumption, but Annie didn't know for sure what she wanted to do about going. When she asked us what she should do, we saw an opportunity for her to be able to stretch her own relationship with God.

"That's up to you, Annie. What does God want you to do?"

"I want you to tell me what to do, Mom and Dad!"

"You're growing up, Annie, and you know Jesus. He'll lead you. We'll be praying for you."

So Annie read her Bible, prayed, called her youth pastor, and considered it all. She decided it was OK to go the concert. She had a great time with her friends, and all was well. Today she points back to that as a signal time in her maturity as a Christian. She had *heard* from God.

Later, as a senior in high school and a talented character actress in the drama department, Annie was offered a leading role in the production of *Blythe Spirit*. But she began to sense that taking the role of a crazy psychic in the comedy was not something that would please the Lord. We did not express a preference one way or the other, but Annie grappled with the issue and prayed about it over an entire weekend. She began to sense that, though she knew what she believed about the occult, and though the comedy was not seriously occult, some of her friends might take her participation as approval for interest in such things. So she went to school on Monday, explained to her drama teacher why she was turning down the role, and contented herself with simply playing a minor role.

How do we usher our children into their own authentic communication with God? The process requires us to gradually turn over to them the responsibility of listening to God and obeying His direction. Our focus isn't to hear God for them and be His interpreter. Instead, we're always looking for the opportunities that will allow them to seek God themselves and make the decisions about His will and His leading. It's a partnership we make with them. We guide

Let It Shine!

them in their interaction by reminding them what they need to do in order to become a good listener. So when kids tell us, "I'm not sure what God wants me to do," here are some directions that we can give them that will lead them into making good choices.

Be asking. Tell your children what James said. "If you need wisdom, ask our generous God, and he will give it to you. He will not rebuke you for asking" (James 1:5 NLT). This is a great place to be thoroughly involved in the process with them. Praying with our kids is an incredible opportunity for parents to teach truth about their relationship with their kids and their kids' relationship with God. They learn that we're concerned about what they're concerned about and, more importantly, that God's concerned about it, too. They learn that their parents can communicate with them and not be judgmental—as long as, of course, we take care to communicate with them and not be judgmental. They learn that God is their source for all things, that He is alive and at work in their lives, and that in all things, we turn to Him first of all.

Here's a word of caution. Resist the temptation to "run the show" here. Let your child lead the prayer, even if you have to do a little prompting. You contribution should be affirming what they have prayed and then praying for them. Don't speak for God, because it just might dilute or even invalidate an important moment in your child's relationship with Him.

Be active. As they search for God's direction one of the big mistakes that many Christians, both kids and adults, make is doing nothing. It's very easy to lose track of all the other important things in life while we're waiting to hear from God. And when that happens, we're paralyzed.

So here's the good news and the bad news. If, when your child reaches their teens, you see that happening, take heart! That means they really are developing a heart to hear God's direction and that they want to do the right things. The bad news is that spiritually, emotionally, and physically, it's not a really great place for them to stay. They have to remain active in their pursuit of God in order for it to be fresh and vital.

Probably the very worst thing you can do is to tell them to just shake it off and move on. We can't lessen the importance of this season with busy work for them to do. We can't just think that if they ignore it, the questions about the future will just fade away. But you can inspire them to do the things that will genuinely bring some clarity to this confusing time in their life. When kids arrive at the point that they sincerely want direction from God, they will eagerly grasp at whatever might bring them some help. And that's where parents enter the picture.

If we tell you here that some kind of "intervention" is necessary, please don't recreate what you would see on some reality show on television. We're talking about something very low-key and under-the-radar. Once again, creative methods provide the most effective means to move kids along the track that God has in mind for them.

They need input from God's Word, but it probably won't connect with them from a pulpit, a Sunday School podium, or around you family's kitchen table. Did you ever hear Charlie Brown's teachers talk on the *Peanuts* television specials? "*Wah wuh wah wuh wah wah wah . . .*" That's how most lectures end up sounding to a teen. So search the Scripture and find pertinent verses and stories, then email or text them to your child with a note that you "thought this might be meaningful to you today." Find some passages from books, mark them, and leave the book on the bed with a note that says, "I'd really like to hear your opinion about this."

One-on-one counsel is important here too. Set up a time to do something with your child that seems very adult—like coffee at your neighborhood Starbuck's or jogging in the park together. In that nonthreatening setting, ask questions about how they're doing. Reinforce the fact that you see them growing up and doing a great job of it. Then listen, and talk very little. If a sit-down with you to discuss a deeply personal matter seems a bit intimidating to them, talk to their youth pastor or Sunday School teacher about spending some one-on-one time with them.

Be available. Working hand-in-hand with activity is availability. For our purposes here, we could define availability as offering ourselves to service and ministry. Throughout this book, we've talked about serving others. In fact, you've probably realized that that is one of the prevailing themes, and it's of utmost importance in partnering with God to raise world changers. During the times when your young person is struggling to hear from God, when focusing outwardly, they may find some clarity for what's going on inside. Encourage your kid's availability and guide them into opportunities to reach out to others. Don't shut any doors on their behalf. Instead, work with them to filter their ministry through their schedule and your family schedule. Make sure that serving others doesn't get lost in the myriad of other responsibilities. And as always, reaching out to others is more effective for your child and those they minister to if you work on the project alongside them.

Growing up is tough. And growing up, while making good choices and determining to follow God, can be even more overwhelming. As we teach our children about hearing from God and walking in His will, let's determine that we will be the voice that will free them from anxiety and allow them to confidently grow in their fellowship with God. Let them learn from us the joys of following Christ. Show them a God who is personal. Show them a God who is concerned. Show them a God who is involved. As we give them the freedom and encouragement to stretch beyond the comfortable, they develop that intimate and authentic interaction with Jesus that releases them to walk His ways with assurance.

Recommended reading:
Hearing God, Dallas Willard
Hearing God's Voice, Henry and Richard Blackaby
Understanding God's Will, Kyle Lake

THINK

▲ Have I sought God's direction in my life enough to be confident in my own ability to discern His direction for me?

▲ If I am reluctant to allow my children to seek God and make some decisions for themselves, why is that so?

▲ In the same way that a child moves from tying his own shoes to eventually driving a car, do I thoughtfully consider an appropriate timeline for transferring spiritual responsibility to each of my children?

DO TRY THIS AT HOME!

❏ A good exercise in identifying the right course of action in life's situations is to use the plots of stories, television shows, books and movies to talk and think and apply Scripture by asking our children, "What would you do? Why?" And then, really listen to their answers.

"I thought He was with you," said Joseph. "I haven't seen Him since we left Jerusalem."

"I've asked everyone I know and nobody has seen Him." Mary was beginning to panic now. "Joseph, where could He be?"

"Just calm down, Mary, and let's think. He couldn't be too far away."

Tears were beginning to well up in Mary's eyes now, and there was a lump in her throat. She was beginning to think the very worst. It wasn't like her 12-year-old son, Jesus, to just disappear. She had assumed that He had been traveling with friends or some of His cousins. But now, on the second day of the long trip back home to Nazareth, He was missing.

As word got out, everyone in their large traveling group began to search for Jesus, but He was still nowhere to be found. The only logical thing for Mary and Joseph to do was to retrace their steps into Jerusalem and hope and pray that He was all right.

Much of the Passover crowd had thinned out by the time they got back to the city. Mary and Joseph hurried down the streets, frantically searching for Jesus and then headed for the marketplace. Many of the merchants had packed up their wares, and most of the rest seemed frazzled and disinterested after several busy days of work there. The distraught parents described Jesus and asked if anyone had happened to see Him around. But nobody could help them.

Finally an older man walked over to Mary and tapped her on the shoulder. "Excuse me," he said. "I couldn't help but overhear you." She turned and looked at him, perhaps the only glimmer of hope she had left.

"There was a boy alone in the Temple when I was there this morning. He could be the one you're looking for."

"In the Temple?" Mary exclaimed. "How long ago?"

"A couple of hours ago," the old man said. "But some of the rabbis there told me He had been there with them for several days."

Mary began to weep as she turned to run to the temple. "Oh, thank you, sir! That must be Him!"

The man grabbed her arm before Mary was able to hurry away. "Just one more thing," he said. "If that's your son, I want to tell you, he is an extraordinary boy. You are to be commended. I've never heard anyone, young or old, who had such a grasp of the Scripture.

He had so many questions that challenged everyone there and made us think. I was barely able to tear myself away…"

Mary appreciated the kind remarks, but she just didn't have any time to waste talking with the man. She called out to Joseph who was at another vendor's cart, questionning, and the two of them rushed to the temple. As they burst into the entrance, they saw a group of men huddled together. They recognized some of them as being well-known and respected men of faith in that community. The discussion that was going on was an animated one, rising and falling in volume, occasionally mixed with joyful exclamations and intense controversies. And in the middle of it all was Jesus.

"Son!" exclaimed Mary loudly. "We've been searching for You everywhere!" She surprised herself and irritated some of the religious men with her boldness there in the temple.

The discussion abruptly stopped, and everyone quickly turned toward her. Jesus stood up, His head barely peeking above the group of men seated around Him. "There was no need to search for me," Jesus said to her. "Didn't you know I would be right here in my Father's house?" His words puzzled everyone around Him. He told the rabbis good-bye and walked over to Mary and Joseph.

With the incident now concluded and Jesus back with His family, Mary sighed deeply. She was relieved, but a bit perplexed. She quietly contemplated what she had seen and heard. She didn't understand fully all that had transpired these last couple of hectic days, but she knew that her role as the Messiah's mother had taken a turn. Jesus was growing up, moving forward in the calling that His heavenly Father had appointed for Him. God's words were personal to Him. She must begin to release her heart for God's mission for Him to save mankind.

(Based on Luke 2:41–50)

CHAPTER 13

Time to Shine

And I am certain that God, who began the good work within you, will continue his work until it is finally finished on the day when Christ Jesus returns.
—Philippians 1:6 (NLT)

Almost every parent has experienced that sick feeling down deep in the pit of the stomach. You're in a store or some other crowded place with your child when you get momentarily distracted. Then you turn back around to the place you last saw your child, and the child is gone! Thankfully, this horrible scenario usually lasts no more than a few seconds before you spot that little one around a corner or behind a fixture. But you never forget how it felt for that one terrifying moment.

The Bible offers very little of the story of Jesus' childhood. In Luke 2, we see the incident in which Jesus' family is visiting Jerusalem and Mary and Joseph become separated from their 12-year-old son. Can you identify with Mary's fears when she discovered that Jesus was missing? The few anxious moments had turned into days, and she was understandably frantic. When she finally found Jesus there in the temple, her words were similar to what any mother's would be. "Don't you ever do this again," she said. "We were worried sick!"

It was at this moment that her son reminded her of what her calling was. "Why were you worried? I was taking care of my Father's business." Nobody really understood fully what the young man Jesus was saying. But it caused Mary to think. And as she did, she remembered that her Son was the Messiah. He didn't really belong to her and, ultimately, she had to seek God for every detail of how to handle these situations that would inevitably arise.

Even though our parenting hurdles seem small compared to Mary's, there are still many of the same issues in this culture and with our kids. Our task as parents is to actually completely release them someday, out of our care and into the hands of God. Letting go is never comfortable. There's that nagging feeling that we might have missed something that we should have taught them or that maybe something didn't really sink in. It seems like only yesterday we brought that child home from the hospital and, now, the child is making decisions about the future and is close to walking out the door. There are times we would like to press a replay button and redo what we did to prepare them. Knowing that is only a fantasy, we still want to intervene and make sure we correct anything that might be lacking. And it's at those times our kids may recoil and accuse us of interfering.

Years ago, there was a memorable television commercial for a pain reliever. The adult daughter, obviously the target of her mother's continual nagging, had contracted a miserable headache. One final suggestion made by her mother absolutely pushed her over the edge. "Mother, please! I'd rather do it myself!" she yelled through clinched teeth. Yikes! We don't ever want a replay of that nasty scenario in our home, do we?

Between the ages of 13 and 21, kids are required to make some of the most important decisions of their lives. The problem is, that's when they are least prepared to do it. But as kids set out to navigate the hormone-driven roller-coaster ride of their teen years, we have less and less influence each day in helping them make these crucial decisions about their education, their choice of a mate, the direction toward a career, and the mission that God has for them. We can only trust God that they will remember the things we have taught them, because this is the time that they're also trying to break free. But that's not a bad thing. It's the natural course of all parent-child relationships because that's the way God has designed it. From the time of their birth, accountability for their lives is in gradual transition from us to God.

As parents, our role is crucial in this maturation process. If it's our responsibility from the very beginning to present that child's life back into God's hands, then it would probably be a great time for us to provide all the answers to you. Unfortunately, that's impossible. Because, each parent, each child and each child's mission are different. And once the breaking away process begins, it literally never ends. The pages turn and each scenario requires a response that, for that season, allows for God's calling to be more fully alive in our son or daughter's life.

> It's very easy to react rather than respond when it comes to our kids.

When an angel appeared to Mary to tell her about the birth of Jesus, she certainly wasn't given all the answers. But she knew God and trusted Him. Her response to the angel's news was, "I am the Lord's servant. May everything you have said about me come true" (Luke 1:38 NLT) She never forgot that commitment before God. Although your situation certainly won't match Mary's, she demonstrated for us attitudes that enabled Jesus to "be about His father's business." They were principles that all parents can utilize to help enhance God's mission in their child's life, for the entirety of their life.

Mary and Jesus in the Temple. Mary's first response when, at the end of her search she found Jesus in the temple, was typical. And although she didn't fully understand His situation, Luke 2:51 gives us insight into a perspective that she probably had to call on throughout Jesus' life. She hid those things in her heart. She was thoughtful and intentional about how she parented Jesus toward fulfillment of His ministry.

Like Mary, we have to continually remind ourselves about our role in making our child missional. We seek God daily for wisdom regarding our relationship, even after that child is grown. It's very easy to react rather than respond when it comes to our kids. Reaction is the result of emotion, and because we love our children so much, we often allow that emotion to drive what we say and do. A response, however, is measured, thoughtful, and filled with godly wisdom. Often, it's not at all what we're feeling. But because we are seeking God for how we can minister to the life of our world changer, and because we have long before decided that we wanted what God wanted for them, we choose to respond.

Jesus was in the "family business" and He has invited each of us to be a part of it also. The unique mission within His kingdom that He has for your children is enabled and enhanced by your finding ways to release them back into God's hands. That only happens when, as parents, we thoughtfully understand our role and intentionally decide to give our children to God.

Mary and Jesus at the wedding feast. "Whatever He says to you, do it." That was Mary's instruction to the servants at the wedding celebration in Cana (John 2). The hosts were out of wine and, in that culture, that was at least an embarrassment if not downright offensive. We're not certain exactly why, at this moment, Mary went to Jesus with the dilemma, but she obviously thought that He could help. She had confidence in Him, and she had confidence in God's work in Him and through Him.

We watch our children grow from tiny new babies, completely helpless, dependent on our care and attention. We see their frailties, their weaknesses, and their challenges. We may have concerns as to whether or not they can handle what the world throws at them. But, especially as they begin to become young adults, we only do harm if we fail to show our utmost confidence in their abilities and God's abilities in them.

Thoughtless words can tear down confidence. Being intentional about what we say and what we don't say to our kids is vital to determining how solidly they mature in their calling. Two of the most powerful phrases that can proceed from a parent's mouth are "you always" and "you never." The words that follow those introductory phrases can be destructive if they point out flaws and failures. When they are followed by words that highlight your child's strengths and talents, they are like vitamins to your child's spirit. They promote an accurate and positive self-image that's a foundation for boldness and courage.

Mary and Jesus at the Cross. Scripture's most heart-wrenching picture of Mary is when she is at the foot of the cross, watching her Son suffer. There were so many questions and a multitude of doubts that were likely going through her mind, as well as the agony of seeing Jesus in the midst of His most painful trial. No doubt, like any parent, she wanted to lash out at someone, anyone. She would have taken His pain if she could. But she was there beside Him, enduring this horrible scene, grieving over what was transpiring.

Life is difficult, and though our children's calling might not bring us to the foot of a cross, there will no doubt be times that we will see them suffer. As they face difficulties as young adults, our intervention will usually not be what's required. What ministers most dramatically to our maturing children is the assurance that we're at their side.

Many times, a person must necessarily face the most difficult things alone. It's part of the maturing process. In those situations, there's nothing that we can do, as a parent, to alleviate the pain or lift the burden. But we must always be where our kids can find us.

There will be moments, like Mary's in the temple and at the wedding feast, when we realize that our role as a parent is changing. And perhaps the most difficult step is the one we take into the background. It's our responsibility to give our children wings and, then, demonstrate our unfailing confidence in them as they pursue their calling and use those wings. We want to build them up to be undaunted in pursuit of their God-given mission, allowing them to go anywhere and do everything that their Father asks, with the assurance of our love, our encouragement, and our prayers as they go. Those paths may take them through difficulties and suffering. And, like Mary at the foot of the Cross, our calling is not to alleviate it, but simply to be available.

As we watch God at work in our children, our reward is observing His faithfulness in using them for His eternal purposes and His glory. From the time they are small, you see glimpses of His work in them and through them. Then you recognize that once-little life is far bigger than you can contain or control. Your child has been called to change their world.

THINK

▲ Am I personally willing to take risks, or to suffer, in order to fulfill what I perceive to be God's calling in my own life?

▲ What is my gut reaction to the thought of my child, as an adult, doing so?

▲ Searching deep within, do I still view my child as belonging to me or as truly belonging to God? Can I trust God to care for my child better than I can?

▲ What qualities do I want to characterize my future relationship with my adult child? Is there anything I should be doing now to prepare for that?

▬ ▬ DO TRY THIS AT HOME! ▬ ▬

☐ When your teen or preteen expresses a dream, whether it is to attend college across the country or to work with the sick and poor in the most dangerous corner of the earth, enthusiastically invite them to sit with you at the computer, and find out all you can about the place, and its needs. Then pray with your children that God will lead them and use them every day of their lives.

● ● ● ● GOOGLE THIS: ● ● ● ●

✎ Anything and everything your child mentions an interest in!

▬ ▬ ▬ LIVE IT! ▬ ▬ ▬

As the subway clatters beneath New York City, Lindsay Reyes is oblivious to the sound of the conductor announcing the stops and to the rush of dank smelling, chilly air that comes in every time the doors open, spilling people out and taking more in.

She is focused on prayer, and the Word, and spending time with Jesus, seeking wisdom, and peace, and strength, and love she can give away.

And she will need it, for in a moment she will climb the subway steps and emerge into the harsh world of South Bronx, where her sixth grade reading and writing students are waiting for her smile and her kind words, often the only ones they will receive all day.

For a girl who grew up in the traditional culture of church and community in the South, Lindsay's job teaching in one of the toughest public schools in New York might seem like an unlikely stretch. But she traces the roots of her concern for "her kids" back to attitudes that she observed in her mother.

"My mom was a believer," Lindsay said. "The great thing about her was the way she felt for those in need and wanted to serve people—all people. From watching her, I really grew to understand the heart of justice, which is the very heart of God. She never judged people because of their lack of money or the color of their skin. In fact, those were the people she prompted me to show compassion for.

"Even living in the South, I really didn't see poverty, but if my mom found out that anyone was being made fun of, she would talk to me about how to treat them. She gave me a strong sense of right and wrong."

Growing up regularly attending church, Lindsay can't remember when she was not aware of Jesus.

"I had a relationship with God. I felt a connection to Him at an early age and would say I knew Jesus intimately," she said. "But I didn't really understand grace until I was in college, where I was involved in Campus Outreach. The woman who discipled me really showed me what it looked like, not just to read the Bible and try to be good, but to use the Word as the foundation for my life."

In her junior year at college, Lindsay became ill with an autoimmune disease that the doctors were unable to diagnose precisely.

"I spent a year grappling with that," she said, "and I had to learn to trust God for healing. During that time, I decided that I wanted to be a teacher so I just moved on toward that, trusting that God had me covered."

"Now, I'm fine," Lindsay continued. "The disease is gone, though no one knows exactly what happened. For me, that has been a proof of why we have hope."

On one trip to New York City in high school, and another just after college, Lindsay fell in love with the city. Attending summer workshops at Columbia University's Teachers College only enhanced the romance. She began to plan and dream of moving there.

"I had my plan," Lindsay said. "I wanted to move to the city, get a job at a really good private school, and then work at Columbia University's Teachers College, as a consultant in the city schools. I saw this as a glamorous job, and I had to have it.

"Then I read *Savage Inequalities* by Jonathan Kozol, that uncovered the injustices in the Bronx. When you get onto the subway in Manhattan, you are in the richest neighborhood, and when you get out of the subway only a mile and a half away, you are in the poorest. It opened my eyes so much to the needs of the kids in the inner city. For instance, 70 percent of the kids suffer with asthma. They deal with that, and all the other obvious things, every day. I just began to realize these kids were the ones who deserved the best teachers,"

Lindsay said. "They deserve the best, but most teachers would never choose to teach in those conditions."

Then Lindsay's mentor at Teachers College quit her job to become a literacy coach in South Bronx.

"She's the best teacher I've ever seen," Lindsay said.

So, when her mentor told her that there was a job open in South Bronx, Lindsay applied.

"I came to do the model lesson, as part of the application process," she said. "I had heard such bad things, that the kids would curse at you and yell at you, but it was nothing like that. They were beautiful—so full of hope. I was immediately drawn to them.

"I was a little scared of the neighborhood because I had never seen anything like it," she explained, "but I decided it was about time I see the world isn't all perfect. As Christians, we can't just focus on our own worlds and Christian communities until we are 'rescued from this fallen world' and get to heaven. Jesus did quite the opposite. He was right in the middle of the oppressed."

The train pulls into her station, and Lindsay gathers her things. Emerging into the sunlight, she covers the blocks to Middle School 223 with an eager spring to her step. Making her way down the cheerfully painted blue and yellow hall, Lindsay unlocks the red door to her room and breathes yet another prayer for her students.

The bell rings, and she stands at the door, smiling and greeting kids who come past her with warm, eager greetings of their own. In the classroom, the students' sense of purpose and level of enthusiasm are tangible as the lesson begins.

As they move through the lesson, one girl sneaks a piece of gum into her mouth, an obvious infraction of school rules.

Lindsay acts surprised at her misbehavior.

"Maya, I have to ask you to spit that out," she says quietly.

Immediately, Maya's body stiffens, and she becomes visibly angry and defensive.

Lindsay smiles at her.

"Oh, did you think I was mad at you?" she asks the girl. "I'm not mad. I love gum, too. I just need you to follow directions. I love you too much to get angry over gum."

Maya's body language relaxes, and she quietly folds her gum into a scrap of paper.

Lindsay goes through each day with a solid assurance that she is exactly where God intends for her to be, partly because things fell so quickly into place for her.

"There was this really great apartment where some awesome Christian girls were living and creating a wonderful community," she recalled. "I thought it would be so great to live there, but they didn't have room. I interviewed for the job, and then the New York City Department of Education called me in Greenville and said I wasn't correctly certified for the job after all."

But that was not the end of the story.

"Then they called me right back," Lindsay said. "They had found another way that I was certified. At the same time, a space in the apartment opened up. I felt that I had unprecedented favor from God. I walked, and steps unfolded before me."

For Lindsay, finding ways to reach kids' hearts has been a process.

"I had no idea what the kids would need from me," she said. "I didn't know that they wouldn't need me to come down hard on them. Every day, people raise their voices at them, give them the 'evil eye,' and tell them to shut up. I realized that's not what they need. That doesn't mean anything to them."

As surely as she knows she is called by God to her mission, Lindsay's days are not without their serious challenges.

"When I feel like I've given everything to my kids, when I have been graced to love them and pour myself out, but they don't appreciate it or respond, then I begin to doubt that I'm a good teacher.

"It's frustrating when I think I've broken through with one, and then they cuss in my face. It's hard not to take it personally and make my love conditional love. But we do that same thing to God, don't we? And He continues to lavish His love on us. So I realized that I can't be walking in the Holy Spirit and react like that," Lindsay said.

"This past week I had a good week with one of my girls, and then she came in, mad at someone else, and threw a chair. In that moment, I wanted to judge her actions, but then I realized she was acting out of hurt," Lindsay said.

"I want to see them being compassionate to one another, and when they're not, I wonder, 'What am I teaching them?'"

In times like these, Lindsay leans on fellow believers in her community group. "There are so many people that I could text at any time during the day, and they would immediately pray."

Because she was the subject of a short video produced by Deidox for distribution to churches and youth groups, parents sometimes ask Lindsay for advice on training their children to have compassionate hearts.

"Make it a point to mingle, to mix with people who are different, so your kids can see it," she advises. "If you say we are all equal, then model for your kids how to love all people. Let them see you value all people, no matter their race or class. But you have to truly love and value them. It has to be real, because kids know fake when they see it."

Inspired by her story, teens want to know how to find their own calling from God.

"Look at your life. See what you naturally love, what you are good at," Lindsay tells them. "Without a selfish heart, ask God, 'How could I use this to serve?' If you haven't seen the face of poverty, go find it. If you are trying to be like Jesus, go to where He's moving in the world."

The final bell has rung, and the last student has left the building.

"A lot of our kids go home to shelters. They go home to homes where they're in charge. They see people shot in front of their apartment door. Life has not been easy for them or kind to them," Lindsay had explained in the video.

"Many of my students haven't been loved well. They've been abandoned; they've been promised things that have never come. They've been promised relationships with their fathers, their mothers, that have never happened, so they're just worn. They're weathered, and they don't trust love.

"On the first day of school, the first thing I tell them is 'I've been thinking about you all summer. I love you already. You may not believe this, but you can't earn my love. You can make straight A's and have perfect behavior all year, or you can get detention three times a week, and I'm going to love you the same.' And then I spend all year trying to prove it."

Now it is nearly spring, and as she packs her school bag and heads for the subway ride home, she recalls a student who came to her from another room and used words about her classroom like "beauty, peace, love, and gentleness." She realizes that these are things from God, and these are things her students desire.

Settling into her seat for the ride home, she sometimes wonders, sometimes doubts, exhausted and worn. But she thinks, "God, you are sovereign and good. And ultimately, this is Your kingdom, and not mine."

Lindsay's story is available on DVD at http://deidox.com/

CHAPTER 14

The Fat Lady Never Sings

Oh, how blessed are you parents, with your quivers full of children!
—Psalm 127:4–5 (*The Message*)

Dan Cook was a legendary San Antonio sportswriter and television sports anchor who always had an interesting way of delivering a story. When our beloved San Antonio Spurs had fallen behind in the NBA playoffs and things were looking pretty bleak, Cook wanted the viewers to keep their chins up. To conclude his sportscast that evening, he brought onto the set a rather rotund soprano, dressed in full opera regalia. "Remember, folks," he said. "The opera ain't over 'til the fat lady sings."

If you're waiting for the diva's grand finale to signal your last act of parenting and the curtain call that follows, you might want to hold off just a minute. There's a pretty good chance that in this opera, she may never blast a note.

For a moment, let's revisit the refinery we introduced in an earlier part of this book. Despite all the difficult, sweaty work that refiner has to do, he very well might never get to witness the final product. The refiner forging steel beams and girders probably won't get to see them create an office building. At a gold refinery, the process that removed the impurities from that precious metal was tedious and didn't offer much margin for error. But the refiner there last saw the gold in an unattractive lump. He didn't see the beautiful jewelry crafted by an artist, the joy it brought when as a ring it symbolized a lifetime commitment.

Just like the refiner, despite the tasks we perform in raising world-changers, we might not have the opportunity to see the finished product. Our role in the process constantly changes as our child grows into God's calling.

So when does this task of training come to and end for us? If we cram all we can into those formative preschool years, does that give us an inside track the rest of the way? Since it's so difficult to handle teenagers anyhow, can we assume that when our kids reach those years, we've probably done everything we can do? How about when we finally get them into college and they are of legal adult age? Surely, we can just cut the ties once they're out on their own, right?

The fact is, we're never finished. The ever-changing process begins with parents' responsibility for every aspect of that brand-new life. It continues into their adulthood, as we hold experience and wisdom that they seek in discovering their God-given mission.

In so many situations where we've met and counseled troubled families and broken parent-child relationships, the most glaring deficiency we've noticed is that parents have quit parenting. Either they have thrown up their hands in frustration at the lack of positive response and given up, or they were tired of the task and ready to focus on themselves for a change.

Most parents with a troubled kid start out with great intentions, with the same plans for their child that we all have, only to see it all fall apart before them. Then their child rebels and rejects parental authority. So Mom and Dad's response is to resign themselves to the "inevitable." Over and over again, we've heard the refrain, "There's just nothing else I can do."

Or perhaps the prevailing situation is quite a bit different than that. The children have been compliant and have stayed exactly on track. Everything seems to be moving right along as planned. The kids are saying the right things and doing the right things; they're active in the church youth group and succeeding at a fine Christian school. So the parents reason that they can afford to adjust the focus of attention from "them" to "me." They sit back, relax, and punch in parental cruise control. Then, suddenly, they're broadsided by a daughter who gets pregnant or a son who's caught with drugs.

In Proverbs 22:6, the Hebrew word for word "child" is a bit ambiguous, but very possibly intentionally so. The original word used in that Scripture is *na'ar*. It can refer to any age from a brand new baby to a young adult. Because the definition is so broad, could it be that our responsibility is an ongoing, never-ending process? Was the author of the Scripture inspired to intentionally leave that open-ended?

It begins with providing for the brand-new baby's every need. Feeding (frequently), changing diapers, and watching over them. Gradually our responsibilities begin to change. We teach them how to talk, how to walk, how to eat big people food and use the potty. Sometimes, as they begin to grow, we wish they would remain innocent little babies. *But God's plan is that they grow in Him.*

Sometimes... we wish they would remain innocent little babies.

Our task isn't finished when our little one is five and moves into that big old mean world. This is the point that we want to protect them from every tough thing that they might face there. We don't like it when someone hurts their feelings, and we feel that we should come to their aid and defense whenever they face a challenge. *But God's plan is that they grow in Him.*

As difficult as it might get, we're not through when they reach 15. They will be pushing and pulling all the while to be grown up, but our job is to gradually relinquish the control for decisions from our hands to theirs. In the midst of the inevitable parent-teen struggles ranging from scratchy conflicts to all-out combat, our instinct is to hammer them back to submission. *But God's plan is that they grow in Him.*

Maybe as young adults they should be completely free of our influence. They look grown up and, hopefully, we've prepared them well enough to negotiate the bumpy ride of life on their own. We watch as they make some decisions where we might have taken a different course of action, and we want desperately to try to make it right for them. We want to stick our noses right in the middle of the fray, instead of standing by as support and counsel. *But God's plan is that they grow in Him.*

God's plan is that the final decisions about our child's life, goals, direction and ministry are not to be made by us, the parents, at all. His job for Mom and Dad is that, from the beginning, we work to transfer that life He entrusted to us back into His hands. From teaching the infant to walk and talk to the place that as an adult, he or she begins a family and starts the cycle all over again, we are preparing our child to hear God, follow His ways, and diligently obey His voice. Within that span of years, God reveals His plans within the heart and soul of that child that He created. As parents, our role is that of a conduit. We are there to provide the primary connection from the Creator to the heart and the mind of the one that He has called.

Through the process of their growing up, it's often difficult to remember that our child is actually His chosen vessel, called for a specific mission in this world. The episodes of childish irresponsibility or the moments of frailty and vulnerability tend to overshadow that big picture. So we get distracted. We get wrapped up in what we have to do to make that child a productive member of society with the potential to be successful. We feel obligated to shield them at all costs. Yet, God is simply saying, "Press through all the distractions of life and introduce them to Me."

The individuality of each child is amazing. Even parents of identical twins will attest to the fact that each child's personality, motivations, and reactions are unique. That's simply because each calling is unique. Far surpassing the array of beauty and majesty demonstrated in nature, God's creativity is even more evident in the lives of people. And, He has equipped your child for a specific mission.

With that as our focus, all the other things that we instinctively do as parents begin to take on their true significance:

We discipline our children, not that they won't embarrass us by misbehaving, but in order that they learn obedience when God speaks.

We teach them and provide the best opportunities for their education, not for the accumulation of knowledge or even to ensure a comfortable lifestyle for them, but that the breadth of their God-given abilities is enhanced for His service.

We nurture them and love them, not because they are our possessions, but so that they can reflect God's character as salt and light to their world.

We live our lives following God in obedience, not so they see perfection, but that they understand the fulfillment that's found there.

And, then, in a span of time that seems to happen much too quickly, they are adults, neck-deep in the challenges of their own world. We hope that we've said the right things, and lived before them as an example of godly character. We no longer have the assignment of stepping in and giving instruction—or even offering our opinion.

But we're not through yet. We maintain open lines of communication with them; we look for every opportunity to encourage them; we lavishly show our appreciation; we assure them that they have our support; we pray for them diligently; and we love them wholeheartedly.

In Psalm 127, David writes about the blessing of children, comparing them to arrows in a warrior's quiver. A warrior's arrows aren't intended to be just a part of his regalia. They're essentially useless until he takes them from the quiver and shoots them, sending them airborne—sometimes far away—to fulfill the purpose for which they were created. And that may be our most important task as parents. We're sharing life with people who can change their world.

Bibliography/References

1. Chapter 1
Video (Internet)
http://www.youtube.com/watch?v=A-TLCmTs2UE
http://www.youtube.com/watch?v=CX4icGkOHYE&feature=related
http://www.youtube.com/watch?v=-2eCmFgx4d4&feature=related
http://www.youtube.com/watch?v=0qbkSCcI5qY&feature=related
http://www.youtube.com/watch?v=0yaF1LtT0tM&feature=related
http://www.youtube.com/watch?v=HgWCLFDVvgQ&feature=related
http://www.youtube.com/watch?v=hH0X3RmTOGA&feature=related
http://www.youtube.com/watch?v=n1JiwQbnBrY&feature=related
http://www.youtube.com/watch?v=NQOPoYB_LHA&feature=related
http://www.youtube.com/watch?v=5i8pY5hQFMY&feature=related
http://www.youtube.com/watch?v=E-lYlF52haM&feature=related
http://www.youtube.com/watch?v=hy0FNknlDj0&feature=related

Duke, Charles, and Dottie Duke. *Moonwalker*. Nashville: Oliver-Nelson Books, 1990.

Telephone interview with Charles Duke (5/15/08)

2. Chapter 2
Panel discussion at Christian Book Expo, Dallas, Texas (3/20/09)

3. Chapter 3
Spurgeon, Charles H. Compiled and edited by David Otis Fuller. *Spurgeon's Sermon Notes*. Grand Rapids, MI: Kregel Publication. 1990

4. Chapter 5
http://thinkexist.com/quotes/dietrich_bonhoeffer/3.html

5. Chapter 6
http://www.barna.org/barna-update/article/5-barna-update/196-evangelism-is-most-effective-among-kids

6. Chapter 7

http://www.christianpost.com/article/20060421/battered-gulf-coast-ready-for-more-graham/index.html

7. Chapter 7

http://www.christianethicstoday.com/Issue/042/Loving%20People%20Into%20The%20Kingdom%20By%20Tony%20Campolo_042_4_.htm

Confirmed in telephone interview with Tony Campolo (1/26/09)

8. Chapter 8

http://en.wikiquote.org/wiki/Benjamin_Franklin

9. Chapter 9

Powell, Mark Allen. *Giving To God*. Grand Rapids, MI: Wm. B. Eerdmans Publishing Co. 2006. p 85

10. Chapter 9

http://gbgm-umc.org/global_news/full_article.cfm?articleid=4486

11. Chapter 9

http://www.archive.org/stream/theworks03wesluoft/theworks03wesluoft_djvu.txt

12. Chapter 10

http://www.forbes.com/2009/02/26/starting-second-career-lea-dership-careers_dream_jobs.html

13. Chapter 10

http://www.christianethicstoday.com/Issue/042/Loving%20People%20Into%20The%20Kingdom%20By%20Tony%20Campolo_042_4_.htm
Confirmed in telephone interview with Tony Campolo (1/26/09)

14. Chapter 11

http://teawithmcnair.typepad.com/

15. Chapter 11

Howe, Neil, and William Strauss. *Millennials Rising: The Next Great Generation*. New York, NY: Vintage Books, a division of Random House, Inc., 2000.

16. Chapter 12

Tozer, A. W. *The Knowledge of the Holy*. Original copyright, 1961, by Arden Wilson Tozer. New York: Harper Collins Publishers. 1992.

17. Chapter 12

bleonline.org/ble.archive/How_the_Lord_Leads.pdf

18. Chapter 14

http://www.mysanantonio.com/sports/MYSA070408_1A_dan-cook_obit_46c9922_html6318.html

Additional Parenting Titles from New Hope:

Setting Up Stones:
A Parent's Guide to Making Your Home a Place of Worship
Martha and Greg Singleton
ISBN-13: 978-1-59669-219-0 • $12.99

Missions Moments 2:
52 Easy-to-Use Missional Messages and Activities for Today's Family
Mitzi Eaker
ISBN-13: 978-1-59669-210-7 • $12.99

Available in bookstores everywhere